I believe the issues addressed ~~...~~ the most important for today's parents – and whether our children are toddlers or teens. I urge you to read it.

ROB PARSONS, OBE
FOUNDER AND CHAIRMAN OF CARE FOR THE FAMILY

Technology is a crucial part of all our lives. There are huge advantages and some pitfalls we should avoid. Katharine Hill addresses these in a very readable way. Using stories from her own family, anecdotes she has been told and drawing on research evidence, she takes parents through the maze of today's technology and the devices our children encounter daily. The cartoons support some of the humorous stories Katharine relates and most chapters have practical suggestions which many people will find invaluable.

This is a subject every parent will need to address, will be addressing or will have addressed. It would be a great book to read as a family or with other parents. Parents can be reassured by this book not to deny opportunities to their children, but to embrace technology with an awareness of the negative aspects which can lie in wait. This is a first-class read, and one which should be on parents' wish lists.

DAVE LUMSDON
*PROFESSIONAL AND ACADEMIC TUTOR,
EDUCATIONAL PSYCHOLOGY, NEWCASTLE UNIVERSITY;
PRINCIPAL PSYCHOLOGIST FOR DBL PSYCHOLOGY*

We might find ourselves feeling fearful, uncomfortable and unprepared for parenting in this digital age, but what we cannot do is remain silent and uninvolved. Years of youth work has shown me how most young people feel oppressed, in some way, by perceived sex pressures that are amplified by technology. We may feel powerless, but the key message of this book is that we're not! What our children need is for us to acknowledge the reality of the pressures in all young people's lives, define our messages and initiate conversations with our children that are factual, sensitive and effective. I'm grateful to Katharine for writing the book that all of us involved with raising children in the digital age need to read.

RACHEL GARDNER
*PRESIDENT OF THE GIRLS BRIGADE ENGLAND AND WALES;
DIRECTOR OF PARTNERSHIP AT YOUTHSCAPE*

The iPhone and my 10-year-old daughter were birthed in the same year. As parents, we are raising her in an exciting but often overwhelming digital landscape, which is why I'm so glad Katharine has written this book. Bringing wisdom and hope in equal measure, Katharine gives parents and guardians clarity and advice to navigate this new 'swipe and like' culture.

IAN HENDERSON
FOUNDER OF THE NAKED TRUTH PROJECT

Left to Their Own Devices? offers invaluable help to any parent wanting to protect and guide their child in the complexities of today's digital world. We cannot leave our children to work it out for themselves. Parents need Katharine Hill's important advice from the word go.

NICKY AND SILA LEE
FOUNDERS OF THE MARRIAGE AND PARENTING COURSES

Katharine Hill has skilfully and sensitively tackled a terribly thorny subject, that can provoke stress-factor-fifty levels of fruitless angst, with razor-sharp insight and unremitting authenticity. This book is a much-needed resource full of solutions, but it is far more than that. It is a true friend who constantly shouts encouragement at you from the sidelines of the parenting marathon.

DR SAMANTHA CALLAN
FAMILY POLICY EXPERT AND PARLIAMENTARY ADVISOR TO LORD FARMER

Katharine gives practical parenting advice on the trickiest topics and it's the kind of wisdom you only gain from experience. You'll hear stories from parents who have faced the same challenges you do, and have come out the other side. Buy this book and enjoy the careful balance of thorough research, refreshing honesty, and the brilliant humour of the illustrations. Every parent needs to know this stuff, and thanks to Katharine and Care for the Family they can!

JASON ROYCE
YOUTH EDUCATOR AND CAMPAIGNER

This book is a must-read for any parent – full of practical wisdom and helpful tips. It is a much-needed guide for navigating the unchartered waters of parenting in this digital age.

SARAH ABELL
AUTHOR; RELATIONSHIPS COACH; FORMER AGONY AUNT FOR THE DAILY TELEGRAPH

When an issue becomes a storyline in a soap opera you know there's a problem! And Katharine Hill in this book grasps all the nettles that families now face in this Internet age. Her book is well researched and brilliantly connected to the digital world. It resonates with the tensions between children and their parents. It is immensely readable. It is warm, funny, serious and compassionate. It will help you download practical advice to make the most of living as a family in the digital era.

THE RT REVD JAMES JONES KBE
FORMER BISHOP OF LIVERPOOL

Katharine Hill is a fount of knowledge on every issue family life throws at you, dispensing advice with compassion, humour and a healthy dose of realism.

ALEX BORTHWICK
PRODUCT MAGAZINE

Left to Their Own Devices? is a really good book. I don't say that very often! It's also a very sane book. My children are in their thirties. When they were young, the Internet hardly existed and a screen, such as they were, was primarily the television. So this book is such an important title, especially for families who are struggling with their children's time on screen.

EDDIE OLLIFFE
FORMER CONSULTING EDITOR OF TOGETHER MAGAZINE

Any parent struggling with the uncomfortable dilemma of how to manage their children's usage of the Internet will find *Left to Their Own Devices?* a very timely and useful book.

PREMIER CHRISTIAN MAGAZINE

LEFT
TO
THEIR
OWN
DEVICES?

LEFT
TO
THEIR
OWN
DEVICES?

Confident parenting in
a post-pandemic world
of screens

Katharine Hill

Muddy
Pearl

First published in 2017 by
Muddy Pearl, Edinburgh, Scotland.

Reprinted 2018 (twice)
Second edition 2019
New edition 2021

www.muddypearl.com
books@muddypearl.com
© Katharine Hill 2017, 2019, 2021.

British Library Cataloguing in Publication Data
A catalogue record for this book is available from the British Library

ISBN 978-1-914553-06-6

Typeset in Minion by Revo Creative Ltd, Lancaster
Printed in Great Britain by Bell & Bain Ltd, Glasgow

To our dear friends Silas and Annie, with thanks for your love and wisdom through the joys and challenges, digital and otherwise, over thirty-plus years of parenting ... and now grandparenting together!

FOREWORD

Somewhat to my surprise, I find that I am the grandfather of five children! Surely that can't be possible? Wasn't it only yesterday that I took Katie (my daughter) to her ballet lesson? I'm certain it can't have been more than a few Christmases ago that I saw Lloyd (my son) put on a sterling performance as the innkeeper in the school nativity play? But, no! The reality is that it was over thirty years ago, and in that time, a revolution has happened: a digital revolution.

Since time began, the role of parents has been to prepare our children to live independent lives. We attend to their physical need for food, sleep and clothing; we give them boundaries to keep them safe, and we seek to instil in them values that will guide them in the choices they will have to make, both big and small, throughout their lives. But parents today also have another task in addition to those I had thirty years ago. As far as I was concerned, issues to do with screen time were confined to whether or not *Doctor Who* was too scary for a 5-year-old who was absolutely desperate to see it! But the world of screens that we live in today presents us with far greater challenges. As parents, we must help our children make full use of all the advantages of digital technology, as well as safeguarding them from the potential dangers.

In this book, Katharine Hill has tackled all the important issues head-on and has given parents a brilliant tool that is full of practical wisdom and advice. Read it now ... and above all, don't leave *your* children to their own devices.

Rob Parsons, OBE
Founder and Chairman, Care for the Family

ACKNOWLEDGEMENTS

This book and the subsequent editions could not have been written without the help and support of so many people. Thank you to Rob Parsons for his encouragement to write this book in the first place; to Sheron Rice, our senior editor at Care for the Family, who added incredible value to the book, and to my PA Jody Jones.

Big thanks to Samantha Callan and Vicky Lavy for keeping me supplied with up-to-date research, and especially to Nick Philps for editing the copy and adding value to the new editions.

I am grateful to Stephanie Heald and the team at Muddy Pearl – it's great working with you – and to David McNeill for the wonderful cartoons.

Thank you to journalist and author Andy Robertson, Reuben Bradley, and Livy and Felix Yeats-Brown for sharing their ideas from the world of gaming.

And as ever thanks to Team Hill – Richard, George, Ellie and Eva, Charlotte, Will, Ezra and Tabitha Caldwell, Ed, Catriona and Finn, and Henry, for fun, laughter, and for providing the raw material for many of the stories and examples. And now for the opportunity to pass wisdom and good screen habits to our grandchildren.

I am grateful to you all!

CONTENTS

Prologue   xvii

1   Living in a (post-pandemic) Digital World   1
2   A Resource to Embrace   9
3   Parenting Styles   17
4   Too Much Screen Time?   25
5   No Face-to-Face Contact?   45
6   'Everything They Do is Online!'   57
7   Gaming   65
8   Social Media, Identity and Digital Footprint   81
9   Pornography   97
10 Sexting   113
11 Online Bullying   121
12 Grooming   129
13 Internet Addiction   135
14 Consumer Culture   145
15 All Kinds of Families – All Kinds of Issues   155
16 'Sharenting' and Role Models   163
17 Teaching Them to Learn to Discern   171

Epilogue   175
Appendix   177

PROLOGUE

The rain is hammering against Alice's bedroom window as she throws her schoolbag onto her bed. She can hear her little brothers squabbling downstairs. It's 7.15pm and already dark, so she draws the curtains. She has a school science project to complete and turns on her laptop. Before getting going, she notices that Karl is online. He is 15. Karl speaks first:

```
Hi Alice. I've seen you on the bus. You're
in the year below me, aren't you?
Yes.
You're very pretty.
Thank you.
Alice, undo the top three buttons on your
shirt. [Long pause]
Like this?
```

And so it begins.

Before we dismiss this exchange as far removed from the reality of our family's everyday experience of digital technology, we may be wise just to pause and do a reality check. If current statistics are to be believed, online conversations of this nature will be taking place right now in children and young peoples' bedrooms across the country. And many parents are concerned not just about the online dangers of sexting and pornography, but also the possibilities of bullying, addiction, gaming, gambling, grooming, the impact of social media and simply the increasing number of hours children and young people are spending glued to a screen.

The digital world can be overwhelming. Gone are the days of a home computer that lives in our sitting room, waiting for us to turn it on and 'go online'; today, our culture lives online. All traditional lines are blurring: 'digital' is no longer a distinct entity from reality;

social media is not something children 'use' – it's become their filter for experiencing the world. AI is increasingly part of our everyday lives. Our devices talk to each other and even predict our actions and desires.

And our experience of technology in the home during the COVID-19 pandemic heightened our concerns. London School of Economics' Professor Sonia Livingstone comments,

> We've moved, I'd suggest, from seeing technology as a valued addition to our lives, to seeing technology as vital infrastructure. And as COVID-19 has made really clear, for young people especially, life is digital by default.[1]

When we meet parents at our Care for the Family events, questions surrounding how to help their children navigate the world of technology and the impact on their emotional wellbeing leave all other topics in the shade. Many parents feel anxious and bemused. Not only do they have no idea what to do, but they don't know where to go to find the answers. A mum responding to a recent Care for the Family survey said, 'It's a minefield. I wish we'd never invented smartphones. It's just made parenting so much harder. Help!'

When my children were growing up, I was often so terrified they might make bad choices that it felt easier and safer to try to eliminate as many options as possible: no Wi-Fi, no screens, no going to that friend's house, no going to that party. But the truth is that although it's essential to put appropriate boundaries in place (and sometimes that means saying 'no'), just taking the default position of limiting their options only makes their world a smaller place.

Parenting isn't really about raising children or even teenagers – it's about raising adults. From their earliest days, we are preparing them for independence: the two-hour session at playschool; their first sleepover; the half-term stay with their cousins; the geography field trip; the language exchange visit to France; the Saturday job; university. Each step leads up to the day when we will no longer be

---

1 Elena Martellozzo, 'Life is digital by default – so what's the impact on young people's mental health?', *London School of Economics*, 21 December 2020, blogs.lse.ac.uk.

'Try to ignore the drone. It's just my dad.
He's a bit overprotective.'

at their side; the day they leave our home and our protection. And for that reason, we must take every opportunity we can to build strong foundations. As parents, it's our job to sow into our children's lives the values that will equip them to make good choices in this digital world. It's a sobering thought, but unless we do that, our child will only be as safe as the least protected child they know.

This book is written in response to the plaintive cry of 'Help!' from the mum who took part in our survey and the thousands of parents who feel exactly the same: help is at hand. Whether you are new parents with little ones or riding the rollercoaster of the teenage years, it is for mums and dads who not only want to 'cope' with bringing up children in the world of digital technology, but to be on the front foot.

Left to Their Own Devices? Confident Parenting in a Post-Pandemic World of Screens will not only give you an overview of parenting in the digital age, but most of all help you take the initiative and give you confidence in it. With strategies and tips that will equip you to protect your children from the dangers, you'll also be able to help them to embrace the wonderful opportunities of growing up in an online world.

CHAPTER 1

LIVING IN A (POST-PANDEMIC) DIGITAL WORLD

She has been my trusted companion now for a number of years. Always by my side, she is loyal and attentive, bringing me what I want at any time of the day or night, and sometimes even helping me discover things I didn't know I needed in the first place. Colourful and interesting, she is great company. It's so easy to spend time with her; in fact the hours slip by without me realizing it. She helps me connect with old acquaintances, introduces me to new friends – and gives me a window into the highlights of their lives. Dressed for this season in fashionable grey she reminds me of my appointments, pays for my coffee, recommends music to listen to and even helps me keep track of my children's whereabouts. And during the COVID-19 pandemic her presence was a genuine lifeline.

Let me introduce you to my smartphone. Since I bought my first iPhone, she has revolutionized my life, so much so that I am not sure that I could imagine life without her.

History tells us that each generation greets new technological advance with caution, and it can take a while for us to overcome the challenges and embrace the change. One scientist said that information overload is 'confusing and harmful' to the mind. We would be forgiven for thinking that this comment was made recently, perhaps in an article about our 24-7 always-on culture, but nothing could be further from the truth. It was said by Conrad Gessner, a Swiss polymath who wrote about the imagined impact of the printing press on society in 1565.

It was ever thus. Socrates warned against the practice of writing, saying that it would 'create forgetfulness in the learners' souls because they will not use their memories'. In the eighteenth century, the French statesman Malesherbes campaigned against newspapers, arguing that printed media would socially isolate readers. And the introduction of radio and television sparked widespread fear that children would stop reading and their exam results would be affected.

Each generation rails against the disruptive effect of new technology on society, while ignoring the fact that similar concerns were voiced with the very technology it is replacing. But the difference with today's technological advances is the sheer pace at which they are developing. In fact, British journalist Robert Colvile has called the time we're living in 'the Great Acceleration'.[2]

Not so long ago, received wisdom for parents was to station the family computer in the living room so they could keep an eye on their children's screen use. Enter Steve Jobs and the smartphone, and this advice was rendered obsolete. It is difficult now to imagine life without that five-inch screen in our pockets enabling us at any time of the day or night to check the weather, track a run, order a takeaway, message a friend – and a million other tasks besides. Digital technology is advancing at such speed that it is taking time for society to adapt to the changes, but adapt it will. As parents, though, time is a luxury we don't have. Our children need our help and guidance *now*, not in five, ten or fifteen years' time, when it will be too late.

In the first two editions of this book, I focussed on the fact that our children were generally ahead of the game with technology, leaving many parents feeling disempowered and struggling to keep up with the pace of change. But the 2020 pandemic shed a new light on this.

Social distancing and national lockdowns led to a surge in the use of digital technology and a dramatic shift in its impact on every area of family life. Bedrooms were converted to offices and living rooms to classrooms; parents juggled homeschooling and home-working; children tapped through online lessons during the day, moving onto their Xbox at night; and grandparents upskilled to become experts on Zoom. It was a steep learning curve for parents and children alike at times, but the pandemic brought about structural shifts in our online behaviour, integrating it into our everyday lives, and many of those changes are here to stay.

2 Robert Colvile, *The Great Acceleration: How the World is Getting Faster, Faster* (Bloomsbury, 2016).

'I'm telling you, this invention will change the world. In a few years we'll be sharing cat photos on a scale you wouldn't believe.'

My own children are now adults and live away, but when they come back, they still treat our house as home. They help themselves to leftovers from the fridge, deposit laundry in the washing basket, and occasionally litter the living room floor with dirty trainers, empty crisp packets, beer cans and dirty coffee mugs. They are residents. They know how our house works and what our values are (tidiness clearly not being one of them). However, when friends join them, even if they have been coming to our house for years, they are visitors, and as such behave differently. They think differently. They ask before raiding the fridge, wouldn't dream of adding their washing to the pile, and take their trainers (and occasionally even their rubbish) home with them.

This idea of distinguishing between visitors and residents has been used by some researchers[3] to illustrate our different motivation for engaging online. Digital visitors use the Internet as a tool – for example, to place an Amazon order, research a holiday, or send an email. They use it to find information or to perform a task without leaving a social imprint online. For digital residents, on the other hand, the Internet is an integrated part of their lives. The web is not a tool but an environment where they can connect with friends or share thoughts and opinions, and where they leave a digital footprint behind them. They see it as a place to support the projection of their identity, a space where relationships are built.

Whether as a parent you identify more as a digital visitor or resident, the pandemic has, without doubt, blurred the edges. Work meetings, parents' evenings, family quiz nights or sessions at the gym … every area of our life moved online. Few parents would now be considered digital technology Luddites, because the pandemic forced them to upskill. But a word of caution: although lockdown pushed many parents into behaving like residents, the jury is still out as to whether there has been a permanent shift in motivation for online engagement. Many engage in a mixture of visitor and resident modes depending on what they are trying to achieve. My best guess

3 Marc Prensky, 'Digital Natives, Digital Immigrants', *On the Horizon*, vol.9, no.5 (MCB University Press, October 2001), pp1–6. marcprensky.com.

'Unbelievable! Eight weeks and 300 miles on foot
through the planet's harshest environment and they
still have a signal!'

is that, for the time being at any rate, the distinction between digital visitor and digital resident will remain.

In my work with the charity Care for the Family, I have the privilege of speaking to thousands of parents. And as well as the everyday concerns that are part and parcel of family life, there has been an exponential rise in the number of parents saying that the impact of the digital world on their children is the issue that keeps them up at night. After a year of lockdowns, these concerns increased still further. It's as if COVID-19 had the effect of holding a magnifying glass to family life. While some of the positive aspects were strengthened, the fault lines were put under pressure. For many parents and children, especially the most vulnerable in society, the pressures became a hundred times more challenging.

As well as concerns about the sheer number of hours their children spend on screens, the issues parents worry about cluster around three areas:

1. Content: what children see online.
2. Contact: who they talk to online.
3. Conduct: how they behave online.

The issues are wide-ranging and include access to pornography, sexting, online bullying, gaming, grooming, gambling, addiction, sites encouraging self-harm and eating disorders, having no time just to 'be', lack of exercise, no face-to-face communication, the insidious effect of image-heavy platforms and the continuous scroll of social media; and the cumulative impact of all of this on their emotional wellbeing. Months of lockdown amplified these concerns, which are now more urgent to address than ever before.

In fact, research on children's digital use during lockdown found that:

- Website and app visits by children aged 4 to 15 were up by more than 100% in January 2021 compared with January 2020.[4]

4 Linda Geddes and Sarah Marsh, 'Concerns grow for children's health as screen times soar during Covid crisis', *The Guardian*, 22 January 2021.

- Seventy-six per cent of 16 and 24-year-olds spent more time on their phones, while 45% increased the amount of time on their laptops.[5]
- There is growing concern about damage to eyesight as a result of the massive increase in screen time. Data from more than 120,000 Chinese schoolchildren suggested a threefold increase in the prevalence of short-sightedness among 6 to 8-year-olds in 2020.[6]
- There is also (of course!) concern over the negative effect on sleep from more evening screen time.[7]
- Finally, the increase in screen time meant a decrease in physical activity for children. In one key study, only one in five children met the WHO Global physical activity recommendations in the early stages of lockdown.[8]

Reflecting on these issues might cause many parents to overlook the benefits of the digital age and run for cover, battening down the hatches, banning all devices forever and insulating their children in an internet-free cocoon in Outer Mongolia. But even if it were possible, this would not be a good plan. It is too easy to make the Internet the scapegoat for the pressures on our children today, and we need to realize that the problem doesn't lie in the Internet itself but in the choices we make in using it.

Although, of course, we need to protect our children from danger, our ultimate goal is not to eliminate all risk from their lives (and therefore all opportunity), but to enable them to embrace the opportunities and manage the risks well. In a world of unlimited choices, our role is to equip them to make good ones.

5 'The Health Cost of Screen Time', *Lenstore Vision Care Experts*, 2021, lenstore.co.uk.
6 Jiaxing Wang, Ying Li, MD and David C. Musch, 'Progression of Myopia in School-Aged Children After COVID-19 Home Confinement', *JAMA Ophthalmology*, 139(3), January 2021, pp293–300.
7 Federico Salfi et al., 'Changes of evening exposure to electronic devices during the COVID-19 lockdown affect the time course of sleep disturbances', *Sleep*, May 2021, doi.org.
8 Viktoria A. Kovacs et al., 'Physical activity, screen time and the COVID-19 school closures in Europe – An observational study in 10 countries', *European Journal of Sports Science*, March 2021, doi.org.

From their earliest days, our job as parents is to teach our children life skills, particularly those that will keep them safe. We teach them how to tie their shoelaces, do up buttons, spell, read, and cross the road. Hours spent running behind a bike teaches them to cycle. Even more hours spent waist-deep in the chilly and over-chlorinated water of the local swimming pool results in them being able to swim. We feel we know how to help them develop skills and manage 'real world' risks because we have personal experience and understanding of them. However, the online world is different. Even though the pandemic meant more time online for parents, our children's experience and understanding of the digital world will always be two steps ahead of us.

For those less at home in the digital world, the terminology alone can be confusing. What is the difference between an ISP and an iOS? Is a troll a creature from Norse mythology or something quite different? Are *console* and *monitor* nouns or verbs? Help! Of course, tech-savvy parents generally have less ground to make up, but for all there is a challenge. As parents, we can try to keep up with the texting shorthand and discover what acronyms such as *omw* (on my way), *smh* (shaking my head), *gtg* (got to go), or more importantly, *pos* (parent over shoulder) mean. But we don't need to be 'experts', and we certainly don't need to be 'cool' and au fait with every type of digital slang (the last thing a teenager wants is a 'cool' parent anyway).

Despite the pace at which digital technology is changing, as parents we shouldn't feel overwhelmed or ill-equipped to guide our children in this area. The Internet is not a tsunami about to engulf us while we stand helplessly looking on. However, there are some things well within our reach that we *do* need to know, including some important parenting principles that will equip us to navigate our children through the online world with wisdom.

CHAPTER 2

A RESOURCE TO EMBRACE

There are undoubtedly dangers (real and imagined) in living in a digital world, but at the outset, let's acknowledge the advantages and opportunities it offers. The many benefits it brings to families, as well as the business world, are something we can celebrate, enjoy and make the most of. And during the COVID-19 pandemic, the ability to connect online threw us a lifeline.

Before the pandemic put a high bar on international travel, my husband Richard and I decided to book a week away together. It was our first summer holiday without our children, but (apparently unable to change the habits of a lifetime) we managed to book easyJet flights in the school holidays. Not only was it more expensive, but the plane was rammed with stressed parents and hordes of small children.

The young mum in the row in front of us seemed to be alternately coaxing and wrestling twin girls into their seats. Amid cries of, 'It's not fair,' she tried patiently to explain that there was only one window seat. The decibel level increased as we took off. It was not proving to be the most restful start to our holiday. However, ten minutes into the flight, the seat belt sign went off and permission was given for electronic equipment to be used. Within seconds, the fracas in front subsided, and for the entire journey the two girls were glued to a game on a tablet. Heaven! And it's not just flights: in-car consoles have made fractious car journeys in bank holiday traffic with endless games of Hangman and I-spy a thing of the past.

Technology can also be a lifesaver in the home. What parent hasn't breathed a sigh of relief when putting a child in front of a screen during the 'happy hour' – 5pm to 6pm – when blood sugar is at an all-time low, sibling rivalry is at its peak, and the fish fingers are not yet on the table.

'Are you posting your dinner on Instagram *again*?'

Digital technology has also brought about what has been called 'the democratisation of learning'.[9] Gaining knowledge and information is no longer limited to how many books are in the home, and gone are the days when harassed parents supervising homework had to trawl through textbooks and dusty encyclopaedias for information about the cacao bean, volcanoes, the Battle of Hastings or the reproductive cycle of the dragonfly. One click on Wikipedia (which my children tell me is now a legitimate source of reference) has changed everything and opened up new horizons.

And online education doesn't have to wait for school days to begin. Numerous apps are available for pre-schoolers to assist early learning and development: songs, stories and rhymes; games to teach colours, numbers and letters; games to encourage tidying up; apps to facilitate sleep; and games that are simply just fun.

Social networks and tools such as WhatsApp, Instagram, TikTok, YouTube, Facebook and Pinterest, to name but a few, facilitate communication between family members and friends, giving a sense of community and belonging. The ability to WhatsApp and text (a great invention for the introverts among us) also pays dividends with respect to family communication – including tracking down wandering teenagers. We will look at how involved we can – or even should – be in our teenagers' online lives later in the book, but the ability to message them when they are out with friends and establish not only their whereabouts but their expected time home has saved many parents an evening of angst. When my children were teenagers and went out 'roaming', Richard and I would ask them to keep their mobile phones with them, turned on and in-credit so we could stay in contact if necessary. It was amazing to us how many times they were apparently in the only nightclub or area of Bristol with no signal! Devices are always at the mercy of the user, but the principle of being able to keep in touch is a huge advantage.

As well as helping parents keep track of errant teenagers, technology enables families to communicate across the miles. We have friends who moved to live abroad and video conferencing

9 Carolyn Whelan, 'The Democratisation of Learning', *The Economist*, 26 September 2014.

has enabled the children to connect with their grandparents in a way that just wouldn't have been possible by landline or snail mail. They have Zoomed at bath time (the children's bath time, that is!), mealtimes and birthday parties. Stuart (the dad) said:

> 'It's not the same as being there in person, but we've now made it part of our weekly routine. Mum and Dad feel more part of the children's lives, and we all feel closer as a result.'

Digital technology has empowered young people with creative tools that our generation could only dream of growing up. When I was young, the idea of becoming the next Spielberg or Scorsese was little more than a daydream; now, teenagers can shoot and edit a feature length film on their smartphone. And rather than recording music on muffled cassette players, aspiring musicians can produce studio-quality albums on their laptops. If we can encourage our children to use their devices to experiment and create, rather than just scrolling mindlessly through social media feeds, the possibilities are genuinely exciting.

Teenagers at a loose end can also find offline hobbies and new interests on the Internet. A friend's child recently got into basketball and can now bore for England on the subject of the leagues. Another child, who was struggling academically, stumbled across a YouTube lesson on woodcarving and whittling, and this has now become his passion. And another friend's child is teaching herself the guitar. All this via the touch of a screen.

In many ways, the availability of digital communication serves our teenagers' developmental needs well. Ninety-one per cent of 12–15-year-olds now have their own smartphone,[10] and more than two thirds of teenagers say that they would rather communicate with their friends online than in person.[11] Most teenagers want to establish their identity, be independent, look cool and impress someone they're

---

10 Ofcom, 'Children and parents: Media use and attitudes report 2020/21', *Ofcom Research*, 28 April 2021, ofcom.org.uk.
11 Betsy Morris, 'Most Teens Prefer to chat Online Than In Person,' *Wall Street Journal*, 10 September 2018, wsj.com.

'No, I'm sure it's fine.
What's the worst that can happen?'

NB Please don't try this at home – it is highly dangerous to use electricity in the
vicinity of water.

attracted to. Messages on scraps of paper hastily passed along the lunch queue or via a friend are a thing of the past – mobile phones and networking sites have simplified the process. For self-conscious teens, on the day the biggest outbreak of acne has appeared from nowhere, or when a tendency to blush is getting the better of them, social messaging makes this kind of communication much easier.

Many young people have a keen sense of justice. They want to make a difference in the world, and digital technology helps them do that. Sponsored walks, swims and silences have been replaced by initiatives with bigger impact. As teenagers, my children were involved in various fundraising activities and awareness campaigns whose ultimate success was largely due to the viral nature of social media. A couple of years ago, I was presented with a phone and was asked by our youngest to record him having an enormous bucket of ice poured over his head for the 'Ice Bucket Challenge'. He then nominated two friends to be subjected to the same treatment and posted it online as part of a viral campaign that raised awareness of motor neurone disease. This same child took part in the 'Cinnamon Challenge' – a dare to eat a spoonful of cinnamon in sixty seconds without having a drink (potentially very dangerous and certainly not to be recommended!). It was a stunt that played into the teenage appetite for fun, risk and adventure, and also went viral on social media.

Another welcome aspect of digital technology is the benefits it can bring to children and young people with additional needs. For children with physical disabilities, technology gives them many opportunities they wouldn't have had: voice adaptive software, for example, can help them answer questions without needing to write, e-readers help those with dexterity problems to read a book without needing to turn the pages, and the ability to change font sizes and styles can help visually impaired children.

Pippa, the mother of Barney, who has Down's syndrome, told me,

'I love it that Barney, who can't read, is able to find the music he loves to hear just by looking at YouTube videos. He feels great that he can do this without me helping him.'

Digital technology can also improve communication for children on the autism spectrum and help develop social skills and the ability to learn. Lyn, the mother of a 3-year-old boy with autism said:

> After months of using my laptop and Android phone to play games, we decided to get him an iPad. Best. Decision. Ever. Yes, it was expensive, but well worth the money and in just two weeks, my son is communicating for the first time with TapToTalk. He is playing games he never had patience/focus/attention for before like match games and puzzles. iPad = Miracle in our house! [12]

Kyle, who was diagnosed with Asperger syndrome, attention deficit disorder and obsessive compulsive disorder, commented movingly on how technology has helped him be able to have friends and conversations:

> It's basically just the fact that you don't have to have a person staring back at you with what you're saying … two to three years ago I wasn't able to talk to people face to face. Like, this right now, I wouldn't have been able to explain anything. I would have been all shy and weird looking. [13]

During the COVID-19 pandemic, the social advantages of technology were brought into particular focus. Social distancing did not have to mean social isolation. Online picnics, playdates and other creative endeavours dreamed up by valiant parents helped younger children stay in touch with their friends, and gaming and messaging enabled teenagers' burgeoning social lives to tick over. An important anchor for many children was keeping in touch with extended family online, including with grandparents who became tech wizards overnight by necessity. Two of our grandchildren were born just before the pandemic, and Richard and I swiftly joined

12 'Technology and Autism', *Autism Speaks*, autismspeaks.org.
13 Jackie Gerstein, Ed.D., 'Using the Internet and Social Media to Enhance Social-Emotional Learning', *User Generated Education*, February 2013, usergeneratededucation.wordpress.com.

the army of grandparents who have regular chats over Zoom. The children are still not yet 2, so it has involved quite a lot of creativity and effort on our part to find ways of holding their interest, but when we were finally able to see them again, face to face, we found that the hard work had paid off.

Despite the closure of the school gates during the pandemic, online lessons prevented the door from also closing on our children's education, as heroic parents became teaching assistants overnight. Reflecting on the experience of juggling home schooling and home working, one mum said,

> 'While, in many ways, it was challenging, I also realize there were some advantages: I could do battle with my inbox, jump on a work Zoom meeting, and keep an eye on our kids' online lessons, all while sitting at the kitchen table with a coffee, still in my pyjamas!'

For children who find the distractions of the school environment stressful, lessons delivered directly to them via a screen was often an overall plus. And in the bigger picture, one other consequence of the move to online learning was that it highlighted the digital divide in our society. This resulted in the much-needed provision of laptops, tablets and improved online connection to disadvantaged communities.

Some activities will, of course, remain timeless (reading stories at bedtime, kicking a ball around in the garden, playing board games and trips to the park), and part of parenting in the digital age is to make sure that we include those things in our children's lives. But at the same time, we must be careful not to look back at our own childhood through rose-tinted spectacles and try to recreate something that is out of kilter with the culture they are growing up in.

We'll move on to the challenges and potential dangers of family life and digital technology, but as is the case with all aspects of parenting, key to how we handle this is how we behave as mums and dads, and our preferred parenting style.

CHAPTER 3

PARENTING STYLES

In the next chapter we will explore one of the big areas of concern for parents: screen time. But before we survey that battlefield, it may be useful to put the coffee on and ask ourselves a fundamental question that will affect how we approach this issue (and many others): *how do I parent?*

John Wilmot, a seventeenth-century poet, has a famous quote attributed to him: 'Before I got married I had six theories about raising children; now, I have six children and no theories.' As a mother of four spirited children, I can identify with his sentiment!

Before our first child was born I was determined to give the important task of parenting my very best effort. I enrolled my husband and myself in antenatal classes, and with a large knitted sock and a rugby ball as a visual aid we were taught all we needed to know about childbirth. We were encouraged to write a 'birth plan'. We could choose a birthing pool, a home birth or the maternity hospital, and we could select which background music to play and the method of pain relief to use; the possibilities seemed endless. The only fly in the ointment was that son #1 had evidently failed to read the plan or, if he had cast his eye over it, had chosen to ignore it. Three weeks early and making an appearance like an express train, he was having none of it, and this set the pattern of things to come. I was soon to learn that parenting has a lot more to it than blindly following the rules with a guaranteed outcome. The small matters of a determined toddler, stubborn 8-year-old, or defiant teenager keen to make their presence felt, can make life more complicated and unpredictable. Even more confusing is when a normally compliant child surprises us with a little rebellion just to prove that they aren't an easy touch and that we shouldn't take them for granted.

But while there are no guarantees, whatever stage of parenting we are at and whatever the issues, there are some tried and tested principles we can apply that will enable us to parent well.

At our Care for the Family events for parents, one of the sessions that mums and dads find most helpful is when we talk about different styles of parenting. And getting the right style in place will lay a strong foundation as we seek to help our children navigate the digital age.

Experts tell us that there are primarily three styles of parenting. Our particular style will be influenced by our own upbringing as well as by our individual temperament and personality, which will give us a bias. And which style we adopt will affect how we approach setting and maintaining boundaries for our children in the area of digital technology.

At one end of the spectrum is the *authoritarian* parent. This parent can be a perfectionist and likes to be in control. There are lots of rules in the home which are enforced rigidly, with strict punishments for anyone overstepping the line. In this home there will be an exact age limit on when mobile phones, games consoles, tablets and laptops are allowed, regardless of a child's individual maturity or interests. There will be a screen policy with unbending rules covering every minute of the day on where and when children can be online and how many seconds a day they can be in front of screens, with no adjustment for age and no allowances for the holidays and special occasions like birthdays. Phones will be confiscated at 9pm each night and locked away until the following morning. Authoritarian parents will micromanage their children's online lives even when it's no longer appropriate, insisting that they follow their 16-year-old on Instagram in order to stay in control.

This sheep and pen picture illustrates the authoritarian style of parenting. The advantage is that it brings clarity; everyone knows what is and isn't allowed, and there is no danger of any ambiguity or misunderstanding. The disadvantage, however, is that children may feel hemmed in and suffocated, with no

'I think I've got my parenting theory cracked this time,
but we're going to have to have one more child just to
make sure ...'

room for individuality, creativity, spontaneity, independent thought or, more importantly, learning.

I have a friend who parents in this way; her home runs with military precision, rules and regulations. A complex chart on the kitchen wall rivalling an Accident and Emergency admissions board on a Saturday night enables her children to earn tokens for minutes online in return for chores completed to her satisfaction. The rules are fixed, with no discussion or family participation, and no allowance for negotiation.

When our children were younger, I would look at this ordered home that seemed to run like clockwork and find myself comparing it to our more haphazard existence. I'd often feel guilty and, if I am honest, a little envious. This was authoritarian parenting in action, and for a time it seemed to work brilliantly.

But during the teenage years, authoritarian parents may be in for a bit of a shock, and my friend was no exception. While outwardly complying with the rules, as they reach their teens, children in an authoritarian home may begin to harbour a growing resentment at being 'controlled'. They will want to flex their muscles and have the freedom that their friends seem to have. With too many rules and regulations, the authoritarian parent may find to their dismay that their teenagers either push back against those rules or, more likely, vote with their feet, preferring to hang out at friends' homes down the road, where life is more relaxed. Rebellion can sometimes come out later in life – and when it does, it is much more traumatic.

At the other end of the parenting spectrum lies the *permissive* parent. Children with permissive parents may well be the envy of

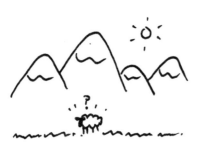

their peers. Their mums and dads are relaxed and laissez-faire, there are very few rules and, even then, few consequences for crossing them. They will have mobile phones, tablets, gaming devices and laptops bought or handed down to them as and when they want them, irrespective of their age. They will have unlimited screen time, what they are watching will not be monitored, and widescreen HD TVs in their bedrooms may well be the order of the day.

The sheep in open country illustrates this permissive style of parenting. Children with permissive parents are free to explore the world wherever it takes them. But while they have plenty of opportunity to forge independence, what they don't have is security. This little sheep looks lost. Boundaries are important – if only to push against – and protective boundaries in relation to the digital world are vital.

The third (and preferred) style of parenting is *assertive*. This is the style to aim for and is illustrated by this picture, where the

 sheep has room to explore but can clearly see where the boundary is. Assertive parents know that setting boundaries are important for a child's safety and sense of security, but they will set as few rules as possible. They choose their battles, saying no to the things that really matter and yes to everything else. Clear boundaries for children are set in the context of relationship (it has been wisely said that rules without relationship lead to rebellion) and there is room for negotiation and manoeuvre on both sides. So parents will have guidelines about the appropriate age for their child to have a mobile phone or other device, but they will be prepared to discuss these with them. They will seek to manage their child's safety while not ignoring the peer pressure they may be under – '*Everyone* else has one … '

Assertive parents will generally allow screen time, but this won't be unlimited – so perhaps no screens at mealtimes or late at night, but with negotiation about this rule in the holidays. This style of parenting is sometimes called 'firm but fair'. The child can see where the boundaries are and so feels (and is) safe. The gate on the paddock is slightly open, and during the teenage years they can exercise freedom by venturing out of the gate knowing it will still be open on their return.

A recent experimental study[14] compared different strategies of mothers to limit their teenagers' use of technology in the home. Assertive parenting was shown to have the best outcomes in terms of teenagers' responses. And it is this assertive style of parenting that will best help us achieve our aims for equipping our children to both navigate the dangers and embrace the opportunities of a digital age.

We'll move on now to look at the main challenges and discover how we can manage them well.

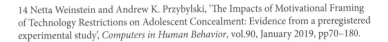

14 Netta Weinstein and Andrew K. Przybylski, 'The Impacts of Motivational Framing of Technology Restrictions on Adolescent Concealment: Evidence from a preregistered experimental study', *Computers in Human Behavior*, vol.90, January 2019, pp70–180.

'Sorry, guys. This is as far as my chain goes.'

'It's working, honey. I have their attention!'

CHAPTER 4

TOO MUCH SCREEN TIME?

Eric Schmidt, former chair of Google, famously once said, 'If you have a child, you'll notice they have two states: asleep or online.' Parents of teenagers may well recognize that description!

The time our children spend on screens can be a battleground in many families. Whether tearing our hair out as our 3-year-old has a tantrum (aka an iPaddy) on being told screen time is over, or attempting to communicate with a teenager whose phone needs to be surgically removed from their hand, screen time can be a hotly contested area. A survey conducted by Care for the Family highlighted that the amount of time children spend on screens is a common concern for parents. One dad told us, 'It just gets harder and harder as they get older and communication gets harder in general. All comments are seen as criticism and lead to rows. I just can't face it, to be honest.'

A layer of complexity was added to the issue in the pandemic when the amount of time our children spent on screens rose exponentially. They diligently (or otherwise) tapped away through online lessons during the day, flopping down in front of the Xbox or chatting with friends on Snapchat into the night. Digital connection was a lifesaver for young people, and many parents had to consider changing their approach to regulating screen time.

As one mum said,

'Enforcing our pre-lockdown screen time rules would have been cutting off our nose to spite our face! Online lessons were the only way to engage with schoolwork, and I wanted the children to be able to stay in touch with their friends. I think before the pandemic we were stricter than some other parents in the amount of screen time we allowed; but lockdown changed everything. It felt like we were just adding to the stress

by piling on guilt about using technology, and in the end, we threw the rule book in the air! Now, as we start to emerge from the pandemic, we are finding old habits die hard and it's a struggle to get back to where we were before COVID in terms of their screen use.'

Screen time starts young: 48% of 3–4-year-olds own their own tablet and 4% have their own smartphone.[15] It is also increasing fast: Ofcom, the communications regulator in the UK, found that pre-COVID, children between 5 and 16 years old were already averaging over six hours of screen time per day.[16] Needless to say, the pandemic exacerbated this trend: website and app visits by children were up 100% at the height of the pandemic; the average daily time spent on apps also rose by 15%.[17]

These figures are concerning for a number of reasons as we'll see below, but where the rubber hits the road for many parents, particularly after lockdown, is the feeling that they are in a continual battle with their children in their attempts to monitor and regulate screen use. Fiona, a mum of four, said:

'We have just come back from a week's half-term, and I am exhausted. Each day was spent using every tactic I could think of to get them off technology and do something else that didn't involve staring at a screen. I didn't want to spend half-term nagging, but that's what ended up happening. They didn't enjoy it … and neither did I.'

Trying to set boundaries around screen use can wear down even the most resilient of parents. Our eldest had an electronic game called 'Zelda' that he particularly liked to play, usually just before the evening meal was on the table. Busy families, overlapping schedules, long working days, shift work, homework, after-school activities, and a teenager's burgeoning social life can make coordinating

15 Ofcom, 'Children and parents: Media use and attitudes report: 2020/21'.
16 'Screen Time', *NHS Greater Glasgow and Clyde*, April 2021, nhsggc.org.uk.
17 Linda Geddes, 'Concerns grow for children's health as screen times soar during Covid crisis', *The Guardian*, 22 January 2021.

'OK, son, screen time is over now ...'

mealtimes a challenge, but we would try to eat together when we could. However, it seemed that whenever the food was on the table, son #1 would be at what he considered the most crucial part of the game. Requests to turn it off and sit at the table would be met with pleas of, 'Just two more minutes …', 'Just one minute more …', 'I'm about to reach the next level, and I can't save it. If you make me turn it off now, I'll have to start again …' Much research has gone into designing games that keep people playing, and succeeding in moving to the next level was always going to be more exciting for my son than the prospect of supper on the table.

As the debate continued, the spaghetti bolognese would go cold and my blood pressure would rise. I would like to tell you that we found an easy-to-implement foolproof method of dealing with this, but at the time, we didn't. Hindsight is a great thing, and there were definitely some strategies we could have tried that might have reduced the angst. Now married with a child of his own, George was at home recently and rediscovered this childhood game. Just the sound of the catchy tune sent those memories flooding back and started to make me feel on edge!

But apart from the effects of children's screen time on stressed-out parents, what are the dangers to the children themselves? While some can manage on less sleep than others, most parents don't need reminding that there is a direct correlation between (lack of) hours spent asleep and grumpiness in the morning!

Before the pandemic, children were already sleeping less than ever before, with a quarter of 11–15-year-olds getting too little sleep.[18] During lockdown, children tended to sleep longer hours, but their patterns were severely disrupted, with 70% of children going to bed later and 57% waking later.[19] Screens are a key factor in both lack of sleep and disturbance to sleep schedules. Though there is disagreement between scientists over the specific biological impact of the blue light emitted by devices, it is widely agreed that using

18 Katherine Sellgren, 'One in four children "has too little sleep"', *BBC News*, 23 January 2020, bbc.co.uk.
19 Sarah Marsh, 'Children's sleep severely affected by impact of coronavirus, say experts', *The Guardian*, 17 July 2020.

phones before bed reduces production of the hormone melatonin, which increases alertness, making it more difficult to relax and sleep soundly. Indeed, given a choice, few children or teenagers would choose sleep over the next game of *Fortnite* or lip-synching their favourite song on TikTok. Yet sleep disturbance in children has adverse effects on physical development, mood, mental health and concentration. Indeed, many schools report that children's work is negatively affected by lack of sleep.

One survey found that children experienced not wanting to go to sleep because they were using social media; over-stimulation meant their minds were still active, and they were frequently woken by their phone bleeping.[20] I have even heard stories of children deliberately setting alarms to wake them through the night in order to check their Snapchat stories or Instagram feeds. Losing track of time when using social media was also highlighted as a factor affecting wider areas of life, including sleep and schoolwork. 'It is routine … going through and checking [social media] before bed'; 'You forget about the time.' And this is exactly what designers and engineers are after: our attention. We live in an attention economy; our biggest commodity is no longer minerals or precious metals, it's our attention – and tech giants are investing billions of dollars to get it.

Research has shown that heavy media multitaskers have greater difficulty in concentrating and find it harder to ignore distractions and irrelevant information, whereas light media multitaskers are more able to direct and focus their attention on their task goal, control their memory and switch from one job to another.[21] Children reported that social media use heavily impacted their motivation to complete homework and revise. Unsurprisingly, the temptation was hard to resist (for most teenagers, there is no contest between quadratic equations and checking TikTok!).

Children also admitted that social media use in class can distract from learning and can affect concentration; Government ministers

20 Fay Poole, 'An exploration of how teenagers' electronic and social media use impacts wider areas of their lives', *Newcastle University*, 2017, theses.ncl.ac.uk.
21 Melina R. Uncapher and Anthony D. Wagner, 'Minds and brains of media multitaskers: Current findings and future directions', *PNAS*, 115(40), October 2018, pp9889–9896.

recently recommended that headteachers ban mobile phones inside the classroom. One study found that banning phones gave pupils the equivalent of an extra week's education over the course of an academic year.[22] Another school found that a 'no phones in the classroom' policy resulted in test results going up by more than 6%.[23] Now that schools have reopened, some learning remains online and even the keenest of students find it hard to focus. Sixteen-year-old Mia commented,

'I'm finding it very difficult to concentrate in online lessons …
I get easily distracted, switch screens, go on my phone more,
open new tabs in the computer.'

Health professionals are aware of the importance of exercise for healthy growth and development; there is growing concern about the lack of physical exercise and levels of obesity among young people. The World Health Organization has described childhood obesity as one of the most serious global public health challenges of the twenty-first century.[24] With more than a third of children classified as obese or overweight by the time they reach the age of 10,[25] it has been described as 'the new smoking'. In fact, if the present trajectory continues, three quarters of the UK population are set to be obese or overweight in a generation,[26] and overweight children are more likely to be overweight adults, with all the accompanying health disadvantages. This is a complex problem and there are many reasons for it, but the effects of a sedentary lifestyle on 11-year-olds who are spending more time on screens indoors (with the opportunity to snack) and less time riding bikes, climbing trees and exploring the great outdoors have to be contributory factors. More

22 Louis-Philippe Beland and Richard Murphy, 'Communication: Technology, Distraction & Student Performance', *Centre for Economic Performance, London School of Economics*, May 2015, cep.lse.ac.uk.
23 Jamie Doward, 'Schools that ban mobile phones see better academic results', *The Guardian*, 16 May 2015.
24 'Taking Action on Childhood Obesity', *World Health Organization*, 2018, who.int.
25 'More than a third of children in year 6 are either obese or overweight', *National Child Measurement Programme England*, 2020, digital.nhs.uk.
26 Baroness Jenkin, 'Britain is eating itself to death and our plan to fight obesity is woefully inadequate', *The Telegraph*, 11 October 2016.

time spent indoors on screens during the pandemic exacerbated this problem. A study by the Schools Active Movement found that 84% of schools identified a decline in children's physical fitness, and 60% thought pupils had gained 'excessive weight' as a result of lockdown.[27]

It all feels like a minefield, but there are some straightforward ways to get started in creating a healthier home environment.

WHAT PARENTS CAN DO

✓ Take some simple, practical steps
Carrie, mother to three teenage girls, told me,

> 'We have a family rule that all our phones are charged downstairs at night. I was having difficulty sleeping recently and went downstairs to get a glass of water. As I went past the kitchen where the phones were charging, I couldn't believe the activity; notifications were rolling – it was like Blackpool illuminations! My girls don't need that by their heads all night.'

Another helpful ground rule is for children to put tablets or computers out of sight when they aren't using them which reduces the temptation to default to picking them up whenever they have nothing else to do.

✓ It's not just about quantity of time
The pandemic made us rethink *how* we view screen time. Paediatrician Jenny Radesky even recommends hitting reset on the term 'screen time' itself. 'It doesn't really describe the fraught relationship between technology and your children.' She says that the focus shouldn't be the duration of time, but *how* we're using technology as part of daily life. Is it helpful or not helpful? The pandemic highlighted that not all screen time is the same – a Zoom

27 Jeremy Wilson, 'Exclusive: "Horrific" impact of third lockdown on schoolchildren's physical and mental health revealed', *The Telegraph*, 10 May 2021.

'Erm, honey, do you realize it's past midnight …?'

call with Granny and Grandpa is very different from watching a film, which is different again from gaming. For that reason, Radesky recommends that parents schedule screen time for different purposes: learning, entertainment, or a catch up with friends.

✓ Be intentional: plan how much time they are on screens

It's great to be able to get half an hour of much-needed peace by putting our pre-schooler or primary age child in front of a screen. But while we catch up with a friend on the phone or do an online supermarket order, it's surprisingly easy to discover that thrity minutes has crept into an hour or more. We have simply overlooked how long they have been there. The point isn't that screens themselves are bad – they can be a lifesaver, but they can also be overused as a babysitter.

I would often try to catch up on emails while our children were meant to be doing their homework and, with one thing frequently leading to another, before I knew it their homework had been done (after a fashion), but I would still be in work mode. While I was making inroads on the inbox they would have seized the moment to play on the Xbox. There wouldn't be anything wrong with the gaming; the issue was that I had no idea how long they had been playing. And while from time to time this was fine, what was not OK was that it was becoming a habit.

In our survey at Care for the Family, 70% of parents said that they set some time limits on their child's online activity. How we regulate that time obviously needs to be appropriate for their age – what works for a 5-year-old would clearly be inappropriate for a teenager, but whatever our child's age there are principles we can apply that can prevent screen time becoming such an all-encompassing and recurring issue.

One word of warning: as the pandemic showed us, this will never be a problem we can solve once and for all. It will be a tension we need to continually manage.

Having some age-appropriate agreed family guidelines for time on screens is essential. Each family is different, and each child is different, so the important thing is to develop a system that works for you and for your family. What's right for you may be very different from what works for others, so you may need to prepare for your children to frequently bring that annoying character, 'Everyone-else's-parent' into the conversation. ('Everyone else's parents let them … [fill in the blank]'.) One parent responding to our survey commented that one of the biggest pressures was: 'Feeling like you can't talk to them about [how much time they are on screens] because you might not be seen to be "cool" or friendly – wanting to be their friend instead of their parent.' The fact that 'Everyone-else's-parent' lets them play on their Xbox/PlayStation/Nintendo until 11pm on a school night doesn't mean that you have to bow to the pressure to do the same. We do our children a disservice if we try and be their 'best friend'. The truth is that parents have to do and say things that best friends are not prepared to do, and as parents we may have to take a hit in the popularity stakes. No-one knows your child like you; nobody loves them like you. They may have many friends, but they only have one mum or dad, so have the confidence to agree some limits that you know work for you and your family.

Involving our children in the discussions and genuinely giving them a voice rather than imposing an arbitrary regime means that everyone is more likely to buy into the agreement. Giving them context can help. So, 'we're going to make sure your game doesn't take up the whole day because we want to do more together' is likely to illicit a more favourable reaction than 'put that Nintendo away!'. And while it's never too late, the earlier you can start to get good habits in place, the better.

The kind of guidelines you can agree when children are 6 or 7 need to change in the teenage years as they set sail with AirPods in their ears and a smartphone in their pocket, on course for increasing independence. While some negotiation with teenagers can take place over screen use in the home, once they are out of the house or at friends' houses it will be up to them to self-regulate the time they spend on screens, so it's worth emphasizing to them that with greater freedom comes greater responsibility. And it is the boundaries that we have put in place over the years and the values that we have sown into their lives that will equip them to exercise this freedom wisely.

✓ Talk to other parents

As mentioned above, most mums and dads attempting to set boundaries at home will have been told about 'everyone else's parents', who are (apparently) much more relaxed in their approach to technology. The best way to discover if this is really true … is to ask them!

The charity PAPAYA (Parents Against Phone Addiction in Young People) was founded by GP Dr Susie Davies as a result of seeing first-hand the negative effect of smartphones and social media on the mental health of a generation of young people. The charity encourages parents to meet together and make informed and positive choices around the use of technology in the home. Not being allowed a smartphone (and therefore excluded from TikTok, WhatsApp or other group chats) can be seen as social suicide. Dr Davies comments, 'If parents can meet together and agree the same boundaries, it can make all the difference.'

One group of Year Six parents agreed to hold off giving their children smartphones until secondary school. Another valiant group of Year Seven parents agreed only to buy their children a basic Nokia phone; others agreed that phones were to be deposited in a basket in the kitchen and not taken into bedrooms on sleepovers. While there may not be 100% buy-in from the group, most parents breathe a sigh of relief when they realize they are not fighting a rear-guard action on their own. And for those parenting alone, having the support of others can be particularly powerful. Be empowered: parents acting together really can change a culture.

✓ Decide on your family values

On a camping trip when our children were small, Richard and I were talking with a family friend who was by then a grandfather. He told us how he and his family had adopted 'the principle of the three Ds' as a framework for their family values. This was a very simple concept of three behaviours all beginning with the letter 'D' that were out-of-bounds for their family. They were:

- **D**ishonesty
- **D**isrespect
- **D**isobedience

The three 'Ds' are like three sides of a triangle, and everyone was free to do anything they liked within the triangle but could not cross over it. Each 'D' was something that was important to them as a family:

- Honesty – so there would be consequences for telling lies or other **D**ishonesty.
- Respect – for other people and their possessions – so there were consequences for rudeness, thoughtlessness and **D**isrespect.
- Obedience – so there were consequences for deliberately being **D**isobedient.

Family values are the principles we live by, and it can be helpful to actually think through what our values are. Individual families will have different priorities, so decide which things are ultimately important to you. We had a number of different values in our family but after hearing about the three Ds from our friend, we adopted them. Although it was a simple formula, it covered almost every eventuality, and when it came to setting boundaries it wasn't a bad place to start. The point about having family values is that they give us something to aim for and impact how we live in all areas of family life – including the online world.

✓ Use screens to enrich family life

Rather than focussing entirely on policing the amount of time our children are spending on screens, we can allow technology to enhance family life – something that many people discovered in the months of lockdown. Our lively family WhatsApp group increased communication and connection between us in ways we wouldn't have thought possible when we were all living under the same roof. Of course, truculent teens may be reluctant to join in that kind of conversation, but be creative and think of ways of using shared technology that they enjoy such as shared playlists or gaming together. We can also use media as a springboard for other activities. One dad bought his children a book about Minecraft which has sparked all kinds of conversations and imaginative play.

It also might help to incorporate screen use in things we might previously have considered a non-screen activity. For instance, one dad told me that family outings with his boys were transformed when he changed his attitude to technology. Instead of telling them to come off their phones and get their coats to go outside, he adopted a different approach. He encouraged them to get their coats, and then bring their phones with them to take photos and videos, and to use Instagram, TikTok or even a GoPro camera to record the afternoon activity.

✓ Draw up a family media agreement

Many families try to draw up house rules about online and screen use called 'family media agreements'; it's a great idea and never too early to start! These are simply guidelines which are in line with your family values that everyone, including parents (here's the challenge!), signs up to. Whatever the shape and size of your family, get some drinks and favourite snacks and make it a fun experience to talk through the issues together. It's obviously easier the younger they are, but even the most combative teenager may cooperate if they think they have a voice and there's something in it for them. You might want to introduce it when your child first begins using technology in the home independently. Some families drew up a special COVID-19 agreement during the pandemic which set out guidelines and expectations for those unusual times. As life returns to some kind of normality, now may be the time to tear that one up and create a new one for the post-pandemic world.

If possible, frame it as 'what is allowed' rather than a list of 'don'ts'. And with the 'don'ts' remember to think through what the repercussions are if someone steps outside the boundaries. Where possible, rather than an arbitrary punishment (e.g. grounding for a month), link the consequences to the original misdemeanour; for example, restricting access to a console or particular app. Let the consequence itself teach the lesson. For families with a range of ages of children, the guidelines will need to be on a scale according to age. The agreement isn't a magic bullet and may be too formal for some, but part of its value is simply in sitting down together and talking these things through.

One family decided to draw up a three-column sheet with 'Yes, we can', 'Ask me first' and 'Don't even think about it', with the rules potentially moving columns as the children get older. See the appendix for links specifically related to family media agreements, but if you want to create your own media agreement, here are some things you might like to consider:

- How many hours a day can be spent using a computer, tablet, smartphone or playing video games?
- Can you schedule screen time for different purposes: learning, leisure, entertainment or a catch up with friends?
- Are there different rules for when friends come round/at weekends/on birthdays/holidays?
- What devices can be used and when? Once schoolwork is finished? At mealtimes?
- Just before bed? Late at night? Bedrooms? (With teenagers, not permitting any use in their bedroom may be unrealistic as they do need some privacy, but the point is not to encourage isolation.) Are social media sites allowed, and if so, which ones?
- What information can be or shouldn't be shared online?
- What films/TV programmes can be seen? What is our attitude to adult, violent or sexual content?
- Are any particular websites off limits?
- Who pays?
- What should your child do if they encounter something scary online or something that makes them feel uncomfortable?

The world is your oyster, but make sure that your children know that the agreement is intended to work *for* your family – a seat belt to keep everyone secure and safe rather than a straitjacket to restrict behaviour. We'll be looking at online safety basics in Chapter 8, and you might like to agree that following these guidelines is part and parcel of your family's ground rules.

As part of the family media agreement, you may also like to install some software on your family's devices to limit time online (see appendix for further information). One valiant respondent to our survey said, 'I have programmed the router to switch off at 11pm meaning that no-one (including us) has access after that time so as not to show discrimination to the children.'

A number of families we know have invested in multi-chargers. They have an agreement that everyone charges their appliances downstairs at night to ensure that they all get a good night's sleep. Highly recommended!

✓ Encourage selective viewing

In a 24/7 screen world, it is unrealistic of us to expect younger children to have the maturity and self-control to ration their own viewing. As parents, we can help by setting some agreed guidelines. On Demand TV can actually be used to facilitate good family time. Try sitting down each week with your children and planning a few programmes to watch together. This is far preferable to them spending hours mindlessly scrolling through YouTube videos, watching things for the sake of it. When used intentionally, platforms like iPlayer, All4, Netflix and Amazon Prime provide the possibility to decide on programmes that everyone's interested in. Agree a time to watch them that works for the whole family.

✓ Use technology to help

There are integrated tools within devices to help us regulate our online lives. An iPhone's screen time feature records the owner's online activity, displaying it in a chart – a sobering experience for many! Apps such as 'Freedom' block notifications, calls and access to distracting websites for set periods of time. And parenting apps making it possible to set screen time limits; children can request more time, which can be agreed or denied as appropriate.

✓ Encourage non-screen activities

When our children were younger, we were given the opportunity to spend a week white-water rafting down a beautiful river and sleeping under the stars at night. We travelled light, and any belongings had to be stowed away in waterproof bags until the evening. We had no mobiles, no screens, no technology; nothing but the river and the incredible scenery we passed each day. If we'd told our children they would enjoy a tech-free holiday, I doubt they would have believed us, yet all four would now say that week was one of the most enjoyable and fulfilling of their lives. The principle I learnt and tried to apply when we were back home was that if, as parents, we can encourage activities that will catch our children's imagination and sense of adventure, even if they don't seem too enamoured at first, they will find it is possible to have a different kind of fun … even without a phone or laptop.

When he was a teenager, one of our sons was excited to be going on a weekend away with his youth club. The kit list came through the week before with essential items to bring – sleeping bag, clothes that you didn't mind getting muddy, a cake, eighties fancy dress – and then there was a PS: 'Please don't bring a phone.' He was incensed. What a 'stupid', 'lame' and 'unfair' rule! What were the leaders thinking? How would they survive? Against all the odds and repeated petitioning from a band of agitated 14-year-olds, the youth leaders held their ground. Returning on the Sunday evening, our son reported that he'd had a 'wicked' weekend and, in a weak moment, even admitted that he hadn't missed his phone.

Particularly at the younger end of the age spectrum, we can't always expect our children to self-regulate, so we need to give them a helping hand, protecting them from the incessant demands of social media and helping them play an active part in family life. I am not suggesting parents become self-appointed outward bound instructors, organizing every minute of their children's screen-free time with high ropes/canoeing/coasteering and other risk-taking adventure activities. Not every child will like outdoor activities, and other options are available. My nephew hates any activity involving a ball, but a bank holiday local drama course enabled him to discover a wonderful talent for acting, and he has gone on to study drama at university. Exactly *what* they do isn't important. The principle is to encourage them to discover even a small amount of non-screen activity that they enjoy.

✓ Understand the teenage brain

In recent years, advances in technology have given us some new information about the changes that occur in the brain during puberty. They are fascinating, and understanding these changes should be compulsory for all parents of soon-to-be teens. It seems that as well as the incredible burst of brain development that takes place in early childhood, there is an equally significant surge of activity in adolescence. In fact, it's all change as the brain goes through extensive remodelling (it's been described as 'a networking and wiring upgrade') to make it much faster and more sophisticated.

This process means that throughout adolescence, teenagers will get better at balancing impulse, desire, goals, ethics, self-interest and rules – what some psychologists refer to as 'the brakes'. It will result in more complex and sensible behaviour, at least some of the time(!), but at other times, especially to begin with as the brain takes time to adapt, things may not go so smoothly. The two parts of the brain that are involved – the amygdala (responsible for emotional responses) and prefrontal cortex (planning, reasoning and self-control) – don't develop in tandem. In practice, the bad news is that many of our teenagers won't get their 'brakes' until well into their twenties.

Consequences and making common sense decisions come second to taking risks and having a good time. This might shed light on the fact that your 16-year-old seems unable to understand your reasoning when you suggest that posting on Instagram until the small hours the night before their English GCSE exam might not be the best idea on the planet!

*'It's not my fault! My prefrontal cortex isn't
fully developed!'*

We were going to visit our children's grandparents in Birmingham for a special birthday lunch a few years ago and had made it abundantly clear to everyone (including our boys) that it was a three-line whip and that we needed to be in the car and on the way by 11.30am at the very latest. (We had a reputation for not arriving on time for family gatherings – one I was anxious to shed.) Our son had been at a sleepover (a misnomer, if ever there was one) the night before, but had promised to be back in good time. At 11am he texted to say they were all playing FIFA, but that he wouldn't be long. 11.15 … 11.20 … 11.30 came and went. I texted to convey my angst and to ask his ETA only to be told, 'k – dw – omw' (which if you need a translation means 'Okay, don't worry, on my way'). Another phone call elicited the information that the score was Aston Villa 0–0 Man City, and the delay was because they were hoping for a result. We were now going to live up to our (clearly well-deserved) reputation for lateness at those particular family gatherings.

I was not happy – a fact which I lost no time in making my son well-aware of. Now, years later, I still think I was justified in losing the plot with him, but I might have approached the situation in a more considered way if I had only understood that this was a demonstration – in real-time – of the teenage brain's susceptibility for fun to trump logic. They are a work in progress!

When she heard about the teenage brain for the first time, one mum with a 15-year-old said: 'It's such a relief to discover. Not only is it not all my fault, but it's not all his fault either!' Just understanding that our teenagers will approach the consequences of time on screens differently to us makes dealing with the issue a whole lot easier.

'Help! My mum's put the childlocks on and is trying
to have a conversation with us!'

CHAPTER 5

NO FACE-TO-FACE CONTACT?

We had family friends round for Sunday lunch. One of the guests was telling us about some writing she was doing on the subject of relationships. In the course of the conversation, she asked our daughter how many 'real' friends she had on social media. The answer: over a thousand. We were open-mouthed – not so much at her reply, but more by the fact that she thought: a) this was normal, and b) these relationships were 'real'. She saw no distinction between 'online' and 'offline' relationships; all these people were her friends whether they were relating to her from behind a keyboard a hundred miles away or sitting next to her in an English lesson.

A lively discussion followed, and as a result we agreed to change our terminology and talk about 'face-to-face' rather than 'real' relationships as, in our daughter's eyes, her 1000+ online friends were every bit as real as the school friends she saw physically every day.

This terminology proved useful during the pandemic. Since lockdown minimized opportunities for face-to-face contact, many discovered new ways of socializing and staying in touch. A concerned dad enquired how his son was managing in not being able to see his girlfriend for weeks on end. His son looked puzzled at the question and reassured his dad that things were fine. They were, he said, in regular communication on Snapchat. In fact, further investigation revealed that he had completed a grand total of 155,915 Snapchats and his girlfriend an astonishing 400,003! In their eyes, Snapchat was just as effective a vehicle for maintaining real friendships as chatting together on a park bench.

While lockdown gave the opportunity for more face-to-face family time, teenagers in particular missed being able to hang out with friends, and many developed new routines, including regular check-ins on different apps. Netflix parties (streaming content together), pre-arranged group Zoom calls, and gaming were all popular ways to catch up with friends. Fifteen-year-old Alice started gaming with a girl she knew from drama classes commenting, 'We've become closer through playing Fortnite together'. Jack, also 15, said gaming was his main form of catching up with friends. He switched his primary console from a PS4 to an Xbox because that was what all his friends used. Most were regularly multi-screening, using multiple devices so they could chat to friends while simultaneously gaming or scrolling through social media.[28]

But while a smorgasbord of devices, platforms and apps have enabled friendships to tick over, few would argue that they have been an adequate substitute for genuine face-to-face connection.

In a recent survey,[29] 87% of young people agreed that they had felt lonely or isolated during the lockdown period and a study of young people in Bristol found that 63% struggled to cope with the reduction in social contact, agreeing that no amount of phone calls or video chats could replace physically being with a friend.[30] In fact, research revealed how lockdown had a 'funnelling effect' on friendships: the narrowing of circles of friends due to the sheer effort required to keep in touch online. This caused some young people to find themselves left out in the cold without a 'bestie'.[31]

Body language forms an important part of our communication, and chatting via a screen means subtle nuances and facial expressions that would normally be picked up are easily lost, increasing the chances of misunderstanding and conflict. However engaging multitasking, multi-screen, multi-app sessions are for our teens, they don't come close to an in-person conversation with another human being or, more importantly, the sheer power of being actively listened to.

And it is not just our teenagers that are affected. Parents have been concerned for some time that screen use is inhibiting our

28 Ofcom, 'Children's Media Lives 2020/21', *Ofcom Research*, 28 April 2021, ofcom.org.uk.
29 Emma Thomas, 'Coronavirus: Impact on young people with mental health needs: Survey 2: Summer 2020', *Young Minds*, July 2020, youngminds.org.uk.
30 Maisie Davis et al., 'Mental Health and Covid-19: In Our Own Words', *Barnardo's*, 2020, barnardos.org.uk.
31 Victoria Gill, 'Lockdown may have lasting effects on friendships', *BBC News*, 26 August 2020, bbc.co.uk.

children's ability to communicate face to face and now schools are reporting that young children's language skills have been impacted.

Suzie Hayman and John Coleman's helpful book *Parents and Digital Technology* has a sobering quote:

> I'm a nursery nurse and one of my colleagues drew my attention recently to a worrying trend. She noticed one child who always looked down at first when you spoke to him, as if when he heard a voice he expected it to come from something in his hands. We realised he's not the only one, and it's the kids whose parents think that iPads and apps on their phones are the answer to a crying child.[32]

If you have preschool children, this conversation may sound familiar:

> ***'Daddy, why can't I have some crisps?'***
> *'Because we haven't got any.'*
> ***'Why?'***
> *'Because I haven't done the shopping yet.'*
> ***'Why?'***
> *'Because I had too much to do this morning.'*
> ***'Why?'***
> *'Because I was busy helping Granny.'*
> ***'Why?'***
> *'Because ...'*

... and on it goes.

On a good day, a 4-year-old's interrogation worthy of a QC at the Old Bailey may be endearing, but when you are tired and hassled this constant questioning can drive you mad. However, annoying as it can be, asking repeated 'Why?' questions is part of a child's natural curiosity and plays an important part in them finding out

---

32 Suzie Hayman and John Coleman, *Parents and Digital Technology: How to Raise the Connected Generation,* (Routledge, 2015), p93.

about the world and their place in it. As they develop language and computer skills, the Internet offers every possibility of helping them gather information. They can google and discover answers to the burning questions of life that leave us baffled: 'Why do we never see a baby pigeon?'; 'Why can't I see my eyes?'; 'How much does the sky weigh?'; 'Does God have a beard?' But invaluable as Google and Wikipedia are, digital answers cannot be enough. It is vital that our young children also have the opportunity for a conversation with a real person. And, more importantly, it is vital that there is someone who can give them the value and dignity of being listened to.

One of the most important theories of child development is known as 'attachment theory'. Professor John Bowlby established that strong emotional and physical attachment to a primary caregiver is critical for a child's development.[33] When parents and carers respond to a baby's needs to be fed, comforted, kept warm or stimulated, the baby learns that they are loved and loveable. The baby will learn that if they cry, the parent will pick them up and cuddle them. They will learn that if they smile, the adult will smile back and vice versa. Through these 'bonds' of attachment they build a map of how relationships in life work. The kind of relationship they have with us becomes a template for their future interactions and friendships, so a strong, loving relationship is vital. Without a secure attachment as babies, in later life people can experience feelings of loss and anxiety, poor self-esteem, and an inability to trust others and form positive relationships.

The amazing thing is that the quality of this nurturing relationship actually affects the physical development of the brain. Sobering pictures demonstrate the shockingly smaller and less developed regions of the brains of children who have suffered severe neglect compared to those of children who have been nurtured and loved. So a positive attachment experience in early life will affect us throughout the rest of our lives: nurture, as well as nature, plays a vital role in brain growth.

33 John Bowlby et al., 'The effects of mother-child separation: A follow-up study', *British Journal of Medical Psychology*, vol.29, no.2, 1956, pp11–247.

Professionals are not yet certain how screen use at an early age can affect attachment, but it must follow that if a baby spends more time in front of a screen than in eye to eye contact with a parent, the bonds of attachment will not be as strong. Similarly, if a parent's attention is constantly focussed on a device, rather than on responding to the needs of the child, strength of attachment might be also affected (a challenging thought during lockdown or other occasions when the demands of work frequently spill into home life!).

The teenage years present a different challenge when it comes to face-to-face relationships. It was week two of our *Parentalk – Teenagers* course, and a group of parents from the local school had come along, some desperate for strategies to use right away, others keen to get ahead for when the teenage season of parenting arrived! The subject that week was 'communication'. I noticed a mum sitting towards the edge of the group. She looked preoccupied and weary, and she was leaning back in her chair as if collecting her thoughts, grateful for a moment just to herself. The evening began and people started to talk about some of the challenges of communicating with their teenagers – headphones on (or AirPods in!) 24/7 being top of the list.

After hearing some of the other parents' stories, this mum felt empowered to share what was happening in her life. She'd been widowed young, and had been left to bring up three young girls. Her oldest daughter was 9 when her father died, and had been a tower of strength to her through the difficult months and even years that had followed. Bright and chatty by nature, her daughter lit up the room when she came in, usually followed by a group of friends, all chatting, laughing and having fun. Fast forward a few years and things couldn't be more different. The bright, vivacious 9-year-old has morphed into a monosyllabic, grumpy teenager. Instead of being her mum's companion and friend, she now won't be seen out with her and makes no attempt to hide the fact that she finds her irritating and annoying.

When she had finished her story, others joined in to relay similar experiences: 'My son won't even look me in the eye'; 'The most I can get out of him is a grunt'; 'She chats away to her friends on the phone, but when I ask her what she wants for tea she bites my head off. I find it so hurtful.' As she listened, the relief on this mum's face was tangible, and she began to cry. She fumbled for a tissue, then looked up and said, 'You have no idea what this evening has meant. Knowing it's not just me has made all the difference in the world. Thank you.'

As we have seen, the teenage years are a time of change and adjustment. When we can't get any response from a 15-year-old who only comes to life when they are on their phone, it's tempting to lay the blame at the door of social media and technology. But the truth is that some of our communication challenges with teenagers are down to normal adolescent behaviour, possibly exacerbated, but not caused by technology. If your child is at that stage at the moment, don't despair – there is hope. As Rob Parsons writes in his book about teenagers, one psychologist likened the teenage experience to the launch of a spacecraft:

> With twelve years or so of training behind him, a pubescent boy makes his way to the launch pad. He climbs aboard 'Adolescent One' as his mother and father bite their nails back at Mission Control. The engines roar into life and Darren makes his way into the stratosphere. And then it happens: they lose all contact with the spaceship. Now and again they pick up what sound like grunts, but nobody can decipher them. The years go by, until a whole decade has passed and then suddenly – signals from outer space! Darren's still alive! And, remarkably, he has discovered the power of speech again. His parents rush back to Mission Control just in time to see the live pictures of his capsule bursting into the earth's atmosphere. All their fears are over. Darren is back! [34]

34 Rob Parsons, *Teenagers! What Every Parent Has to Know,* (Hodder, 2009), p9.

WHAT PARENTS CAN DO

✓ Make face-to-face contact with our children

If the way we interact with our children in the early years can actually impact their brain development, it goes without saying that eye-to-eye contact, smiling, cuddling, playing and tickling will trump time alone in front of a screen every time. Life is busy, and every family has its challenges, but we can try to make the most of those moments while we can.

I increasingly see phone holders attached to everything from bikes to buggies. Having baby equipment that accommodates digital devices is a useful option (especially if it helps to distract a fractious toddler in the supermarket queue), but not if it discourages face-to-face interaction with our children and prevents us from talking and pointing out trees, dogs, caterpillars, pretty leaves and butterflies on walks to the park.

I was recently visiting an old friend to have a cup of tea together and catch up on life. Noticing the time, I had just got up to leave when she suggested we could have another twenty minutes together if I came with her to collect her children from school. It had been a while since my youngest left primary school, but old habits die hard and waiting outside the classroom felt strangely familiar. However, one thing that was strikingly different was the number of parents on mobile phones, quickly grabbing a few moments to catch up on social media. At 3.15pm prompt, the doors opened and Class Three surged into the playground in a sea of blue sweatshirts. One girl in particular caught my attention; she was waving her painting and calling, 'Mummy, Mummy! Look! Look! LOOK!' This mum was dressed in a black suit and stiletto heels and was engaged on the phone on what seemed to be a work call. To her credit, one look at her daughter's eager face made her decide that matters of company budgets and strategy could wait – there was more important business to attend to. She ended the call, bent down (quite a feat in those heels), cupped her daughter's face in her hands and said, 'Darling, that's a lovely painting. Tell me all about it.'

It's not just 5-year-olds that need face-to-face contact. Teenagers need it just as much but *on their terms*, that is, at the most inconvenient times of the day or (more usually) night! Be alert. It's certainly not always easy, but we need to be ready to grab what scraps of face-to-face communication we can. It will be worth it.

We can seize moments for real conversations during the everyday routines of family life such as when we're with our children in the car (a great one for teenagers) on the school run, and especially at mealtimes. I remember trying hard not only to eat together as a family when we could, but to have mealtimes as a screen and mobile-free zone, even when our children's friends were round. An opportunity to encourage conversation was a game we played called 'High/Low' when we would take it in turns to tell each other the high and the low of our day. The children didn't always cooperate, but just occasionally we would hear of a goal scored in a football match, a falling out in the playground, a good mark for a history essay or a mean Instagram post – things I doubt we would otherwise have found out about.

Everyday moments of communication may be lean in the teenage years (so take hold of them when they come your way!), but it's also possible to create them intentionally. At Care for the Family's parenting events, I often talk about a routine that Richard and I developed when our children were quite young. In order to have some one-to-one time with each child, one of us would take one of them out to Tesco for breakfast on a Saturday morning. With four children, it meant they got a turn once a month, and they could choose which of us they wanted to go with. After a while, as I waved my husband off for yet another breakfast, it began to dawn on me that he seemed to be the companion of choice – I hardly ever got to go! Why didn't they want to come out with me? Was I not a fun mum? Feeling a little insecure, I made some enquiries. This is what I discovered: breakfast with me involved Weetabix, smoothies and toast, but breakfast with Richard included chocolate eclairs and cheesy wotsits all downed with a bottle of coke. I realized at that moment that this exercise wasn't about healthy eating. Important as their five-a-day was, it could be overlooked on Saturday mornings in order to create a fun time that they looked forward to and that gave both them and us the opportunity to talk and to listen. The conversation would rarely be deep and meaningful. We would chat about the latest FIFA game (always a struggle for me) or hair braids (more of a struggle for Richard), but, especially in the teenage years, there were some precious moments of screen-free connection where we could chat about the important things of life and allow space for them to share their hopes, their fears and their dreams.

Those Saturday morning visits to Tesco have laid a foundation in our children's lives. They're now all young adults and live away, but they still seize the chance if home to take one of us for breakfast.

✓ Encourage our children to give others face-to-face contact

As well as creating face-to-face communication with our children, we can encourage them to give it to others. If visitors come to the house, it's not a bad idea to insist that our children press the pause button on their device – just for a couple of minutes – to look up, give eye contact, and say hello (even if they really don't appreciate Aunty Hilda who wafts in smelling of lavender and insists on telling them how much they have grown). It is one small way that gives the message that face-to-face communication really does matter.

✓ Encourage opportunities for one-to-one relationships through online activity

Let's not ignore the fact that the digital world gives children the tremendous opportunity to engage with others of the same age whether at home with siblings, at a friend's house, or at school. Collaborative online learning at school, preparing a presentation with friends on Zoom, making a film or playing multiplayer video games can all help develop communication skills.

One of the advantages of living in a student city when our children were younger was the ready supply of willing babysitters. A procession of hungry students were only too pleased to spend an evening in a warm house with some home cooking in exchange for looking after our tribe. The children themselves had their favourites

'**Wow**. *Well done, Dad. You won* **again!**
You're **so good** *at computer games.*
I don't know **how** *you keep beating me so easily …*'

(one was not asked again after rationing them to one small slice of chocolate cake and insisting they switched channels and joined her in watching *The Antiques Roadshow*). Top drawer by a long way was an engineering student called Charlie. Charlie wasn't interested in *The Antiques Roadshow*, and he let them eat chocolate cake until they felt sick, but best of all he played computer games with them. They would be desperate for us to go out just so he could come round.

Seeing how popular Charlie was, Richard and I followed suit and started trying to play computer games with our children as well. But we were hopeless and while they humoured us, it wasn't much fun, for them or us. I finally came to terms with the fact that I was never going to be as dexterous as our children on the PlayStation (although

I gave them a run for their money on the Wii). But we discovered that a close second to actually playing the games with them ourselves was to be interested in what they were doing and talking face to face about what was going on. Being involved in that way in their screen activities kept our channels of communication open.

As long as appropriate safeguards are in place, online communication also gives opportunities to make new friends. I was recently staying with my sister for the weekend. I arrived, took my suitcase upstairs, came down for a cup of tea, and was surprised to be greeted by three young Norwegians propping up the kitchen units and looking very much at home. My nephew came in and introduced me to his Scandinavian friends who I assumed were here on a school exchange. I was quickly corrected. These were his gaming friends; they had met online and had come over for the weekend to cement their friendship face to face.

'It's Daddy's TV time now – I've been bored at work all day. Off you go and be bored in your bedroom.'

CHAPTER 6

'EVERYTHING THEY DO IS ONLINE!'

It was a Friday morning and I was in the doctor's waiting room. A message flashed on the screen to apologize that appointments were running late. In that moment, almost every person in the room put a hand in their pocket or dived into their bag and produced a mobile phone. There was an unsaid agreement: if we were going to have to wait, we would make the most of every second. I checked my family WhatsApp group and others caught up on emails and messages while the child next to me scrolled through YouTube prank videos on his mother's phone. As I waited for my turn, I reflected on the hours I'd spent waiting in that room over the years with the range of ailments that beset young families, and, in the absence of digital entertainment, the fidgeting and wrestling that would take place while waiting for our name to be called.

But however welcome videos and games are in occupying fractious children in waiting rooms, the availability of 24/7 entertainment does mean that our children are seldom offline. (And if they are, it is probably because there is no signal, or their battery has just died.) With young children, imaginary games using whatever props are around them and make-believe stories encouraging creativity and adventure can all too easily be usurped by the beckoning swipe of a screen.

Perhaps more importantly, the 24/7 'always on' culture means that our children have no time to be 'bored' or even just to 'be' (and this was exacerbated during COVID lockdowns). A newspaper article encouraged its readers to 'Lean into boredom, not your smartphone screen'.[35] The truth is that if we can learn to embrace boredom rather than reaching for our phone or tablet in every idle moment, we can

---

35 Gayatri Devi, 'Boredom is not a problem to be solved: It's the last privilege of a free mind', *The Guardian*, 28 September 2015.

discover more about ourselves and the world around us than we would think possible, and we can encourage our children to do the same. The teenage years in particular are a time of self-discovery, and phones can distract our teens from the psychological work of being an adolescent: mooching around, learning about themselves and finding their place in the world – a vital stage that was curtailed during lockdown.

During the pandemic, our children had days on end of unstructured time which it was all too easy to fill with digital entertainment. An Ofcom study found that in lockdown, many teenagers spent a large amount of time online, usually alone in their rooms, binge-watching Netflix and gaming.[36] These were unusual times and in reflecting on our children's online habits in that season we should perhaps cut ourselves (and our children) some slack. Rather than piling on the guilt, expecting homes to have been screen-free seed beds of innovation and creativity, most parents need to be congratulated for simply getting everyone through.

At least once during the (pre-lockdown) school holidays one or more of my children (and even, horror of horrors, all four of them) came out with the words that cause every parent's heart to sink: 'I'm bored!' It's so easy to respond to this by springing into action and providing some form of activity, digital or otherwise, to keep them fully entertained.

Perhaps it's because we feel like we're failing them if they are bored, or that boredom is a 'problem' we have to solve. But psychologists say that quite the reverse is true: 24/7 activity can be counterproductive, and far from being a bad thing, some unstructured time is important for a child's healthy development.[37]

In his infinite wisdom, Winnie the Pooh once said, 'Don't underestimate the value of doing nothing'.[38] Wise words

36 Ofcom, 'Children's Media Lives 2020/21'.

37 Kenneth R. Ginsburg and the Committee on Communications, and the Committee on Psychosocial Aspects of Child and Family Health, 'The Importance of Play in Promoting Healthy Child Development and Maintaining Strong Parent-Child Bonds', *Pediatrics*, vol.119, no.1, January 2007, pp182–191, pediatrics.aappublications.org.

38 Siobhan McNally, 'Winnie the Pooh Day: Best quotes from the loveable bear to make your day brighter', *Mirror*, 18 January 2019.

'I really don't know where you find the
time to put your "busy" badge on ...'

from a bear! But many of us lead busy lives: we have family responsibilities, demanding jobs, endless to-do lists, and can't imagine the luxury of being able to do nothing. More and more of us are growing accustomed to living in the fast lane; it has become a way of life. 'Busy' is worn as a badge of honour. We tweet in the supermarket queue and catch up on emails while waiting for the kettle to boil, but the only problem is that those we live with, especially our families, also get caught up in the vortex. While home-working-home-schooling parents hardly had time to draw breath in lockdown, for others the disruption to our usual routines gave a welcome moment to pause, to draw breath and to take a hard look at the things that are important to us and how we spend our time.

As parents, we are the pacesetters in the home. Our children take their cues from us. Hard as it is, we may need to take a long look at our priorities and make some tough calls. Do we fill our children's week 24/7 with activities that educate and entertain? Or do we allow them time to be bored and to switch off from the bombardment of the outside world? What example are we setting them with regard to our screen activity? Do we allow ourselves time to dream, time to imagine, and time to discover gifts and talents? We don't have to be budding Picassos, emerging J. K. Rowlings or embryonic Mozarts to benefit from boredom; it seems that just letting the mind wander is beneficial for everyone's emotional wellbeing. Research has shown that if we engage in some low-key undemanding activity without concentrating on anything, we are much more likely to come up with creative ideas[39] (which may explain why many of us have our best ideas in the shower!).

Writer and actress Meera Syal relates how she spent the school holidays staring out of the window and doing various things outside her usual sphere – like learning to bake cakes with the lady next door. Out of boredom, she began writing a diary and she attributes

39 Claudia Hammond, 'What happens when your brain wanders?', The Anatomy of Rest, *BBC Radio 4*, September 2016, bbc.co.uk.

'It seems more like ANTI-social media to me.'

this to her writing career: 'It's very freeing, being creative for no other reason than that you freewheel and fill time'.[40]

Unstructured time gives children the opportunity to explore ideas and interests, imagine, invent and create. If our reaction to 'I'm bored' is to fill their time with activities, they may never learn to identify and respond to inner 'calls' that can develop the interests and passions that make life so meaningful. Whether it's baking, drawing, cycling, making a short film, helping out at an animal refuge or doing crafts, their interests and talents can only develop when we give our children the freedom and space to pursue them.

WHAT PARENTS CAN DO

✓ Check the pace you are setting your family

As restrictions lift can we press the reset button and ask ourselves what pace we are setting in our home. Is it sustainable and, more importantly, does it give our children time and space just to 'be'?

When our children were at primary school we found that, without realizing it, we had stepped onto a fast-moving conveyor belt of afterschool activities: Brownies, Cubs, swimming, football, judo, guitar. Most of these involved a car journey in rush hour traffic, and then there was homework and music practice added into the mix. It was a way of life we had slipped into – and it was unsustainable. Wise words from a friend enabled me to regain a sense of perspective, and the following term I cancelled almost all of those activities. It didn't give me the 'mother of the year' award, but in hindsight it was one of the best parenting decisions we made. The frantic rhythm of our family life settled down.

And, of course, part of setting the pace in family life is not just about our children's activities but our own. Parents are often worse at filling gaps with digital activity, and we can actively set a visible example of valuing offline activity or time just to be.

40 Dr Teresa Belton, 'How kids can benefit from boredom', *University of East Anglia*, 2016, uea.ac.uk.

✓ Give your children some space

When our four were of primary school age, the often-wet summer holidays would sometimes feel very long, and I would run out of ideas to keep them entertained. A friend with children the same age had a different approach to the challenge. It seemed that every day she would be packing up a picnic and going swimming or heading off to an adventure park, the cinema, a castle or museum. Her schedule for the children was packed and her energy amazing. With the very best of intentions, she would give me leaflets about activities in the area and encourage me to plan ahead like she did.

Feeling I was letting our children down by not following suit, I remember packing up a picnic one day, loading the car and setting off. The day wasn't without incident! The highlight for the boys (although it reduced our daughter to tears) was when I was stopped by the police for entering a yellow box before the exit was clear. Within minutes of our arrival there were a series of unwelcome events: son #1 pushed his brother into a pile of stinging nettles (no tube of antihistamine in sight in our car, but my friend, of course, had a first aid kit handy); my youngest filled his nappy on a little train miles from the car park, asphyxiating the rest of the carriage; we had to queue for hours for the face-painting (worth the wait for the lion but not the butterfly); and all four voiced their extreme disappointment that our picnic was inferior to the spread my friend had laid on. Despite all this, we had to admit later that it had been a fun day (and one for the memory banks!) but not one that I had the energy or resources to arrange every other day of the holidays. I looked at my friend's action-packed regime and felt so guilty. And there were double measures of guilt the following week when my children declared they were … bored.

I've now come to see things a little differently. As we've discussed, boredom isn't all bad – in fact it presents a wonderful opportunity. Parents have a role to play not just in making that space in the schedule, but also not being too hasty to rush in with ready-made solutions. If our children are younger we may need to provide some materials (some sticks, a ball of string, a rug, a bag of flour, a balloon – the simpler and messier the activity the better!).

If they are initially stuck for ideas we can always give them a challenge to get them going, something to encourage curiosity and imagination – a scavenger hunt, an obstacle course, a story to perform, a den to make, a song to sing. If we allow our children time to be bored the options are endless.

Teenagers too will benefit from taking a break from the 'always on' stimulus of external entertainment and the need to fall back on screens to keep boredom at bay. This is undoubtedly more difficult to manage as they get older, but just creating the space for it to happen is a start. We all tend to be 'busy', and we all use the twenty-four hours allocated to us each day with none left over. The key is in what we choose to be busy with. And if we can choose wisely, not just for us but for our children, our whole family can discover the benefits of slowing down and creating the space just to 'be'.

CHAPTER 7

GAMING

My phone beeped with a notification. It was announcing the next message in a conversation I had begun with Nour, from the city of Homs in Syria.

> **Nour:** I heard some blasts. Are you okay?
> **Me:** Yes, I'm good. I'm at the shop right now. Where are you?
> **Nour:** Still at the hospital.
> **Me:** We're trying to figure out where to send ambulances.
> **Nour:** They're talking about it on the radio; it's in Talbiseh.
> **Me:** Doesn't your sister work there?
> **Nour:** She does ... I'll keep you posted.

I well remember my initiation into the world of gaming. I had been talking to gaming journalist Andy Robertson about the big concerns many parents have, and he suggested I try downloading the game *Bury Me, My Love* on my phone. I will never forget that first experience.

In this game of interactive fiction, I am Majd, who lives with his wife, Nour, in Syria. Bombs have been falling for years, but when Nour's younger sister is added to the list of casualties, Nour decides she must leave Syria for Europe; I help her prepare. We buy two smartphones to keep in touch. She jumps on a truck, I give her a hug and whisper a Syrian farewell – 'Bury me, my love' – in her ear. And so, her adventure begins.

The story is told in real time via a series of text messages between Nour and Majd. Early on, she reports that there is trouble at the border, and her driver is demanding a risk premium of $25,000 to

'You're kidding me! String? You want me to play with string?
Seriously – where's the iPad?'

drive her to Beirut. What should she do? This is the first of many heartbreaking challenges, and on each occasion my response (in this case 'you have no choice' versus 'get another cab') will determine the next stage of her journey and how her adventure unfolds.

While gaming will never be my leisure activity of choice, I still remember being surprised at how enjoyable it was. The game was educational, compelling and fun. I was gripped by the idea that this young woman's fate pivoted on the decisions I made. But after an initial flurry of messages and activity, there had been radio silence from Nour, and I was beginning to wonder if something had happened to her. That night, Richard and I sat down for our evening meal, and as I took the lasagne out of the oven, I heard the unmistakable 'ping' of a notification. We have a 'no phones at the table' rule, but I couldn't help thinking, 'It's Nour! She needs me!' I heard myself say to Richard, 'Back in a sec ... '

This experience has changed my perspective on gaming. The ecosystem of gaming is obviously far bigger and more complex than my week-long foray into *Bury Me, My Love*, and I regularly speak to parents who have genuine concerns about the effect of gaming on their children's wellbeing and its impact on family life. Depending on our background, personality and experience, parents can feel out of touch with their children's all-consuming passion for gaming; just keeping up with the conversation can be a multi-level challenge. We have other priorities, and it is easy to see video games as either too complicated or too juvenile for genuine grown-up interest. We fail to grasp that they are an entirely new medium. They have great potential for storytelling, emotional engagement and education, with all of the beauty, joy and sadness of books, films or theatre. Andy Robertson comments:

Along with the games I love playing with my children, where we compete and laugh and team up, I've played games that have taught me about the power of the wind, what it's like to lose a child to cancer, and the emotional challenge of travelling from Syria to Europe as a refugee.

Parents can play an important role in anchoring these experiences in the context of family life – coming alongside and helping children navigate and make sense of the narrative for themselves. Video games can transport children to magical lands, seed imagination, inspire competition and tell stories in new ways. They can offer unique ways to tackle difficult subjects like bullying, loss or illness, as well as celebrating success, understanding love and learning about respect and resilience. But for this to happen, parents and carers have an important role to play.

While boys tend to play video games more than girls,[41] gaming is not an exclusively male preserve. One Dad told me how he used video games to stay connected with his 15-year-old daughter. They chose a game and worked through the series together:

> 'She has two brothers who tend to monopolize the TV with their gaming, so we plan our Father/Daughter time, and she really looks forward to it. Unlike watching TV or a film together, when chatting is an interruption, gaming is more interactive. She is relaxed and chats away; there is an ease about our conversation.'

I was profoundly moved to hear how a game had brought comfort to my sister's children in the months after their father died. They were celebrating my nephew's birthday, and decided to get out the Wii Sports – a game they had often enjoyed playing together as a family. On commencing the archery, they found my brother-in-law's customized Mii avatar, 'Champion Archer', was still stored on the game, boasting the highest score. The rest of the evening was spent trying to beat him – a feat still to be achieved!

In a similar vein, a young widow spoke of how her husband used to play rally games with their son on the Xbox. The fastest lap in the game (achieved by the dad) is still recorded on the game as a 'ghost driver'. This young boy was able to spend many hours on his Xbox,

41 Cuihua Shen et al., 'Do Men Advance Faster Than Women? Debunking the Gender Performance Gap in Two Massively Multiplayer Online Games', *Journal of Computer-Mediated Communication*, vol.21, no.4, July 2016, pp312–329.

racing his father's ghost car, bringing back reassuring memories of his dad and their special times together.

A quick note on the fast-growing and lucrative industry of esports (electronic sports). Esports are organized multiplayer video game competitions, usually between professional players. The competitions are a spectator sport – online or at live events. Esports enthusiasts argue that the training and intensity required to be a professional is comparable to that of traditional athletes; top players have lightning-fast reaction speeds and heart rates which can match those of sprinters! And esports' legitimacy is increasing: the IOC has decided that it will be included in the 2022 Asian Games. Watch this space; at your next parent-teacher evening, becoming an Esport player may even be included as a possible career option!

At their best, video games can help children develop social and emotional skills, as well as decision-making and empathy. During the pandemic, gaming was the single most popular online activity, with many using it as a way to catch up with friends. Well-designed games can hone critical thinking, planning and evaluation, and can even be a way to form real-life friendships (see the example of my nephew's Norwegian friends who popped up in Chapter 5). But while these arguments will all be useful weapons in the armoury of a teenager seeking to play more FIFA, it's worth taking time to think through some of the issues around gaming so that we can help our children to game responsibly – getting the best out of it, while avoiding the pitfalls.

Screen Time

One of parents' main concerns can be the sheer amount of time children spend on screens, and the disruption this can cause to family life. It is perhaps unsurprising to discover that 90% of 13–18-year-olds in the UK play games online.[42] A study from the Douglas Mental Health Institute in Canada found that video gamers

---

42 Parentzone, 'Skin gambling: teenage Britain's secret habit', *A Parentzone Report*, June 2018, parentzone.org.uk.

now spend a collective three billion hours per week in front of their screens. In fact, it is estimated that the average young person will have spent some 10,000 hours gaming by the time they are 21.[43]

Jack, 16, was interviewed as part of an Ofcom report to gain insight into the media lives of children during lockdown.[44] He had broken his leg shortly before lockdown, so was unable to go out cycling as he normally would. Instead, he spent long hours in his room gaming and was in the middle of a nine-hour relay race on the racing game 'Forza' at the time of the Ofcom interview. He was playing to such an extent that his grandmother offered him £500 as an incentive to leave his room for mealtimes. His mother reported that he didn't do this, so he didn't get the money. She was initially worried about how long he was spending gaming but relaxed after talking to other parents and realizing their children were behaving similarly. In the end, she insisted he leave the house every three days as a compromise.

The issue of managing screen time in general is covered in more detail in Chapter 4, but some parents will be concerned that a child may have developed an actual addiction to gaming.

Addiction

Dramatic, attention-grabbing headlines like 'How screens turn kids into psychotic junkies'[45] have the potential to instil fear in even the most relaxed parents. Despite having been around for decades, there is still no widespread agreement on the impact of video games (both positive and negative) on children's lives. We read headlines of 'conclusive' scientific proof that games are addictive, but the truth is, the jury's still out.

What we do know is that playing video games affects the brain. Dopamine is the neurotransmitter released when we do something pleasurable – it activates and reinforces our brains' 'pleasure

43 Science Daily, 'New light on impact of video gaming on the brain', *Douglas Mental Health University Institute*, May 2015, sciencedaily.com.
44 44 Ofcom, 'Children's Media Lives 2020/21'.
45 Dr Nicholas Kardaras, 'It's "digital heroin": How screens turn kids into psychotic junkies', *New York Post*, 27 August 2016.

pathways'. Dopamine is sometimes called the 'sex, drugs and rock 'n' roll' neurotransmitter. It is released when people drink alcohol, take drugs, have sex and – perhaps unsurprisingly – play video games; if gaming wasn't enjoyable, dopamine wouldn't be released. Any parent hearing that both video games and cocaine activate the same neural pathways will, of course, be alarmed. However, it's worth noting that researchers have found the level of dopamine triggered in the brain by gaming is only about a tenth of that triggered by a chemical substance.[46] (See Chapter 13 for more on addiction.)

Gaming *can* be addictive; the World Health Organization recently added 'gaming addiction' to its classification of recognized diseases.[47] However, before you pick up the phone to make a hospital appointment for your Fortnite-obsessed 15-year-old, it is worth pausing to check out the criteria. To be diagnosed with an addiction, a child must be playing video games for many hours to the detriment of school, personal hygiene and relationships. Not only that, but they must continue to play for twelve months after these problems have been identified.

Researchers have found that gaming addictions are most likely to occur in people who are depressed or stressed, and who use gaming as a method of escape.[48] Certainly gaming was sometimes a welcome distraction to children who were feeling anxious and frustrated during lockdown. If we are concerned by our child's antisocial gaming, rather than jumping to conclusions that they are suffering from a clinical addiction, it is worth pressing the pause button, stepping back, and asking ourselves if this behaviour is masking other issues or challenges in their lives. Excessive gaming might actually be a helpful symptom revealing underlying issues in our children's well-being, rather than the cause of obsessive behaviour.

46 Peter Gray, 'Sense and Nonsense About Video Game Addiction: What does research really tell us about the brain effects of video gaming?', *Psychology Today,* 11 March 2018, psychologytoday.com.
47 World Health Organization, *2017 11th International Classification of Diseases (ICD),* (BenBella Books, 2018).
48 D. Loton et al., 'Video Game Addiction, Engagement and Symptoms of Stress, Depression and Anxiety: The Mediating Role of Coping', *International Journal of Mental Health and Addiction,* 14(4), 2016, pp565–578, eprints. qut.edu.au.

I recently had a wonderful conversation with a 14-year-old gaming enthusiast called Reuben. He told me that when he was young, he loved playing Lego online, but has now moved on to more complex games. He plays between one and three hours a day in a gaming room – not his bedroom – and stops playing an hour before bed (his choice). 'I love the fact that when you're gaming, you're free from the limitations of life. I can do things in games that I couldn't get away with in real life.' I asked him if he was ever tempted to do some of these things in real life, and quickly wished I hadn't. 'Of course not. Nothing on the screen is real – it's just a visualized image'.

He did admit that his mum worried about the impact of the violence in some of the games he played, but he assured me – in his opinion – that he was old enough and that the graphics weren't 'too gory'. I think his mother may beg to differ.

The most compelling part of our conversation came when I asked Reuben what it was he loved about gaming: 'The stories', he said. 'Being able to shape a story; changing the storyline with your choices, finding out about the different characters and plots.' He said that games gave him ideas and helped him with his writing; I was impressed.

I hear many parents talk about the frustration of putting a meal on the table, only to find that at least one member of the family isn't able to come as they are in the middle of a game. Reuben's comment on this was fascinating:

> Parents don't always understand that you can't just abandon a game at a second's notice. It's not like taking a break in the middle of a game of UNO or Monopoly. There are penalties if you give up – it affects your online ranking and reputation. If you are playing with friends, they are depending on you – you would be letting them down if you just left the game. I just need to know in advance if my mum needs me to come for something, otherwise it's difficult.

Money and Gambling

The conversation turned to money. Reuben said he would save birthday and Christmas money to buy 'add-ons' to games so he could finish a storyline or have access to new characters. If he wanted a fun, expensive add-on, he would find a way to earn the money. The issue of online spending is of growing concern. Seventeen per cent of 12–15-year-olds who responded to an Ofcom survey[49] said they had accidentally spent money online, and during the pandemic, parents reported that in-game spending increased by a third, particularly among boys.[50]

While many games can be played for free, in-app purchases can also be made to help players progress through the game; it is these costs that catch us unawares. Debs, a mum of four, told me how her son had run up a three-figure sum on her credit card in this way. In-app purchases are how 'free' games are paid for – a salutary reminder that nothing in life is really 'free'. One 13-year-old boy commented:

> 'I've got my own bank account, so whatever money is in there I don't really ask [my parents], I just spend it. There's loads of £2 or £3 micro transactions that I do all the time that can add up to a lot, but they don't really know about that. They know I'm spending it; they just don't know what on.'

One dad told me that his son wanted to buy a motorbike as an add-on for his game. Doubtful that this was a good use of money, his dad gave him a list of some more worthwhile things he could do with £12. The father's wisdom fell on deaf ears. His son went ahead and made the purchase … and the dad sat back to see him learn a lesson the hard way … if only! Nothing could be further from the truth. In fact, his son was thrilled with his purchase which gave him hours of entertainment.

49 Ofcom, 'Children and parents: Media use and attitudes report 2018', *Ofcom Research*, January 2019, ofcom.org.uk.
50 Internet Matters, 'From Survive to Thrive: Supporting digital family life after lockdown', *Internet Matters News and Opinions*, 2021, internetmatters.org.

A more concerning aspect of gaming is the grey area between monetized add-ons, and actual gambling; 'loot boxes' are a recent example. Buying loot boxes is like collecting football stickers in 'blind' packs: a player pays money to open a box containing unknown items to use in the game. The risk is that the box contains items worth less than its price, or a duplicate of something the player already owns. Loot boxes are popular, (forty percent of children who play video games buy them), but recent research[51] has found that they are 'structurally and psychologically akin to gambling.' Games use 'psychological nudges' to encourage people to buy them, such as the fear of missing out on limited-time deals, and researchers have established a worrying link between buying loot boxes and more serious gambling behaviour. There has been a growing call to recognize them as a form of gambling. As yet, no laws have been made in the UK but there is increasing awareness that features like loot boxes are gambling in disguise.

A Parentzone report recently highlighted the related issue of 'skin' gambling. Twenty-seven per cent of secondary school children had heard of skin gambling; 10% had gambled skins in some form and 29% considered it a 'very big' or 'fairly big' problem.[52] 'Skins' are virtual items that change the appearance of a character or weapon. They are usually cosmetic and don't affect the outcome of the game but increase social standing. Just like owning the latest pair of Nike trainers, one 15-year-old told me that owning a rare skin 'makes you feel cool'. Due to their popularity, a marketplace has developed for the trading of skins which have themselves become an online currency. More worryingly, unlicensed and unregulated betting sites can be accessed without age verification, allowing children to gamble their skins and even gamble money in online casinos, virtually unchecked. One 14-year-old boy from the Parentzone survey said:

51 James Close and Joanne Lloyd, 'Lifting the Lid on Loot Boxes', *Gamble Aware (University of Plymouth & University of Wolverhampton)*, 2 April 2021, begambleaware.org.
52 Parentzone, 'Skin gambling: teenage Britain's secret habit', *A Parent Zone Report*, June 2018, parentzone.org.uk.

I've got a friend who tried one of the websites. He has a huge collection of skins … £1,000 worth. He put £1 on it just to try it out … he lost and wanted to get it back. He lost again and wanted to get his £10 back. He ended up winning £750, but he's really addicted to it. He's 15.[53]

Ultimately, features such as loot boxes and skins may be regulated, or even legislated against, but sadly this won't solve the problem. As tech journalists observe, designers are already looking for other 'gambling-like mechanics' that can be used in new games. It looks like the blurred lines between gaming and gambling will remain. The only solution is to help our children navigate through the ever-evolving world of gaming; to discuss their games with them, and to help them make good decisions.

Stranger Danger

Gaming has a strong social element. A quarter of children aged 5–15 said they played games online with or against people they did not know or had not met in person.[54] Games used to be separate from social media, but the distinction is blurring fast. To most children, interactive games and social media are the same thing.

We need to be aware of the potential for unmoderated chat features to be used by predators to lure children away to different platforms. This makes it vital to understand what is happening on our child's screen, rather than just limiting the time they play. All games have settings to limit how players can interact with each other online, but this requires a little research. Googling the name of the game and 'parental controls' is a good way to find out more.

Although it's a challenge, gaming journalist Andy Robertson's advice still holds true:

---

53 *Ibid.*
54 Ofcom, 'Children's Media Use and Attitudes: 2020/21'.

'The best way to keep things safe is, where possible, to play together and keep gaming screens in shared family spaces. That way we not only see what's going on, but our children have a chance to discuss their experiences with us as they happen.'

Violence

Over the past thirty years there has been heated debate over the link between playing violent games and aggressive behaviour. The truth is, as yet, unclear. A large-scale 2019 study by the University of Oxford found *no* relationship between aggressive behaviour and playing violent video games. However, researchers did find that games provoked angry feelings in players, which manifested in 'trash-talking … and trolling'.[55] In 2018, US scientists analysed twenty-four studies on gaming and found that young people who played violent video games *did* become more aggressive over time. The changes were not big, but not inconsequential.[56]

Dozens of studies can be found to support either side of the debate. What does seem apparent is that playing violent games *can* influence a child's thinking, emotions and expression. Douglas Gentile from Iowa State University sums it up: 'It's not the biggest [link], it's also not the smallest but it's worth paying attention to'.[57] Helpfully, every UK game has a PEGI (Pan European Game Information) age rating which also provides information on content, with descriptors like Violence, Horror, Sex and Language. Setting good boundaries regarding these ratings, noticing our children's reactions to the games they're playing and encouraging them to be self-aware, should create a safe gaming environment.

55 Andrew K. Przybylski and Netta Weinstein, 'Violent video game engagement is not associated with adolescents' aggressive behaviour: evidence from a registered report', *Royal Society of Open Science*, February 2019, ncbi.nlm.nih.gov.
56 Anna T. Prescott, James D. Sargent and Jay G. Hull, 'Metaanalysis of the relationship between violent video game play and physical aggression over time', *Proceedings of the National Academy of Sciences of the United States of America*, vol.115, no.40, October 2018, pp9882–9888, pnas.org.
57 Melinda Wenner Moyer, 'Yes, Violent Video Games Trigger Aggression, but Debate Lingers', *Scientific American*, October 2018, scientificamerican.com.

WHAT PARENTS CAN DO

✓ Join in

Parenting a child who loves video games is in some ways no different from parenting a child who loves Lego, football or reading. The best way to encourage them is to experience it yourself, and then play an intentional role in helping them get the most out of their hobby.

On a day when the inbox is overflowing, the hamster is missing and our teenager has missed the last bus home, this can feel too big an ask. But with the right information and a small amount of time, parents can find games they want to play themselves, opening the door to a firsthand understanding of what they have to offer. Particularly if our children are young, being involved in their games is a great way to gain respect and authority in their eyes, and will mean they are more likely to look to us to guide their playing habits as they grow older.

Andy Robertson tells the story of a mum who called him in distress, feeling she had lost her 13-year-old son to gaming. Andy encouraged her to come alongside her son in his hobby and introduced her to the adventure game *That Dragon, Cancer*; a true story taking players through the highs and lows of a couple's journey with their son's cancer. She began playing and became gripped by the experience. The next night she stayed up until the small hours playing. The following week, Andy received a message from her, thanking him; she had her son back and was part of his world again.

Mats Steen was born with Duchenne muscular dystrophy. During the few years before his death, he hardly left his basement flat in the family home. His father remembers going past the flat during the day, seeing the curtains drawn and feeling sad at his son's lonely existence. They longed for him to have friends. Imagine their surprise when a large group of young people arrived at the funeral – people who didn't know him as Mats, but as 'Lord Ibelin' from the online planet of Azeroth. They had come to say goodbye. Mats' father reflected, 'We used to worry about him staying up late into the night. In retrospect we should have been more interested in the game world where he spent so much time'.

Mats wrote movingly about his online life before his death: 'In the online world, a girl wouldn't see a wheelchair or anything different. There, my handicap doesn't matter … I can be whoever I want to be.' I found that so moving. It was as if Mats was saying, 'In that world I can move and jump; I am the same as everyone else'.

Think about creating a context for playing a game that is situated in the family. Rather than simply using limits or bans that push gaming outside the family circle, playing together helps children anchor these experiences and learn to evaluate them like they do other parts of life.

✓ Agree boundaries

If you have never set age-appropriate boundaries, or the ones that were in place have slipped (which many families found to be the case during lockdown!), you might want to consider calling a truce – gathering everyone together and seeing if you can agree on some breathing space in order to reset gaming habits. Age-appropriate gaming guidelines for your family can be part of your family media agreement (see Chapter 4).

While this may not be easy with a 16-year-old established gamer, younger children often respond well to being asked how often and how long they want to play for, leading to them seeing the self-imposed limits positively. Try helping your child to plan ahead: if the macaroni cheese will be on the table at 6.30pm and it's now 6.10pm, encourage them to pause, and ask themselves the question: 'Do I really have time to start a game that might be difficult to stop?'

PEGI ratings are a helpful guideline for which games are age-appropriate for children to play. Both video games and Esports should carry them, and they are easily accessible online. Responsible Esports organizations will request a date of birth in order to watch online.

✓ Use technology to help

You can set automatic limits on a child's playtime in a number of ways. All modern consoles – Xbox, PlayStation and Nintendo Switch – have parental control features that enable you to limit how long they can be played each day; the game automatically pauses after that time.

There are other routes to achieve this via the Internet connection; your Internet provider may offer settings to limit access. Better still are devices like software like Circle, Qustodio or Kaspersky, or screen time features included in iOS and Android phones, that enable you to set bedtimes, limits and off-times on different devices. These can also limit game time while still allowing a child to access websites for homework.

✓ Talk to your children about money

Chat about how easy it is to spend too much and the dangers of gambling. When they are younger, if they want to spend money on in-app purchases, help them save and spend wisely. Having secure passwords on any account that your child may use will avoid any unwanted or unplanned purchases. Without these safeguards, we may as well log into Amazon and then hand over the controls to our child to fill the basket at will. It is also possible to set limits on transactions or use gift cards to ensure that children understand their spending and are behaving appropriately.

✓ Know your child

Recognize that for some children, playing video games can be a way to relax. Kim, mum to Bradley, said:

> If he's being difficult, my initial reaction is to ban all gaming. However, I have come to understand that sometimes his behaviour is because he's tired or simply had a bad day at school; letting him play on his game for an agreed time helps him unwind.

For some parents, all this can feel a bit overwhelming. But take heart: parents are best placed to notice any change in a child's behaviour after playing a particular game, and to take appropriate action. And be aware that as well as the content of the game, it may simply be that the intensity has caused an adrenaline rush. In the same way that we may need time out if our favourite football team has won (or lost) an important match, we can build in space to help children transition back from the intensity of the game to the reality of day-to-day living.

✓ Encourage other activities

Introduce and encourage other non-screen activities (see Chapter 2) like board games, table-top games, new hobbies or sports, and make them part of family life.

While there may be days when it is tempting to lock all the video games away in the cupboard and throw away the key, there are actually many benefits to families playing together. Provided that parents understand how gaming works, they can be a valuable part of family life.

CHAPTER 8

SOCIAL MEDIA, IDENTITY AND DIGITAL FOOTPRINT

Social media plays a big part in our children's lives today: they use it to share photos and videos, message each other, chat, play games and meet new people. It's fun and engaging, giving opportunities to make connections, build friendships and be creative. And during the pandemic, social media has enabled children to stay in touch with friends and family, with platforms such as TikTok and Twitch dramatically increasing in popularity.

One mum reflected, 'My son has a group of friends who spend a lot of time playing and communicating with each other online. Staying in touch with this community is extremely important to him and is a big part of his wellbeing and identity'.

Rachel Bishop, who advises the Government on online safety adds a note of caution:

'Being online can be a hugely positive experience for adults, children and young people, however it also presents a risk of harm and there is growing concern about the relationship between technology and the mental health of children and young people.'

As parents, our role is not to deny our children these positive opportunities but to protect them from the possible negative aspects, and using the networks' own guidelines regarding age limits is something that can help us in the task. Even though most social networking sites have a minimum age of 13 (and these restrictions are set to tighten),[58] 5% of 10 and 12-year-olds have their own

---

58 Mark Bridge, 'Social media: New code stops children clicking "likes" on Facebook', *The Times*, 15 April 2019.

account[59] and 18% of pre-schoolers have used social media.[60] Perhaps this is because some parents feel that age-restrictions don't matter too much, but it's worth remembering that that in having their own social networking profile, our child will not just have access to that particular site's content; they will be invited to sign in via that profile to other sites. In addition, recent research has highlighted that significant numbers of children have been negatively impacted by social media use: according to Ofcom 2020, more than half of 12–15-year-olds said they had some form of negative online experience. The most likely to be cited was 'being contacted by a stranger online who wanted to be their friend' (30%).[61]

An NSPCC report elaborated further:

> These experiences range from trolling to online stalking, to being asked to send a sexual message. While most of these children were able to recover from what they encountered quickly, around one fifth felt upset or scared for weeks or months after the incident occurred. A fifth of those who experienced something that upset them told us that they experienced this every day or almost every day. Furthermore, the evidence indicates that these upsetting and frightening experiences are not merely an extension of what is happening in the playground. Worryingly, children reported that over half of these experiences were caused by strangers, people they only knew online, or they did not know who caused it.[62]

It has always been the case that an important part of growing up involves young people flexing their muscles, discovering who they are, and establishing their identity as separate from us, their parents. But the big difference for our children today is that they must also

---

59 Ofcom, 'Children and parents: media use and attitudes report: 2020–2021'.
60 Children's Commissioner, 'Life in "Likes"', *Children's Commissioner Report into social media use among 8–12-year-olds*, 2018, childrenscommissioner.gov.uk.
61 Ofcom, 'Children and parents: media use and attitudes report: 2020-2021'.
62 Ruth Ball, Claire Lilley and Heather Vernon, 'The Experiences of Children Aged 11–16 on Social Networking Sites', *NSPCC*, 2014, library.nspcc.org.uk.

do this in a digital world; a world that not only judges them on what they look like but presents a distorted view of reality. Society feeds them the lie that they are what they own, their value is in what they look like, and their worth lies in the number of 'likes' they have on Instagram. Mixed with the consumer pressure to buy, buy, buy, these messages are a potent cocktail for our teenagers.

The selfie culture reflects one aspect of this pressure, encouraging our children to constantly document who they are through photographs: 'I post, therefore I am.' It's all too easy for them to end up comparing their behind-the-scenes life with everyone else's showreel on social media and the pressure to look perfect (with a six-pack/thigh gap/'hot dog' legs/tiny waist/big bottom/big chest/ doleful eyes, or the current 'thick-thin' body shape) is immense.[63] This need to be liked and accepted is combined with the stress of exams, and the desire to have a boyfriend/girlfriend and to get a job.

Many of us may remember that heart-sinking feeling of arriving at school on Monday morning, and realizing that we were left off the invitation list for a party that took place over the weekend. Now, young people don't have to wait until Monday morning: they can sit in their bedroom watching the event unfold in real-time, selfie by selfie.

The online world gives young people an unprecedented opportunity to establish their identity. They can experiment with new ideas, causes and memes all behind the safety of the screen. But as well as allowing them to define and build their identity, it also allows them to *redefine* it – to write a new script. There is the possibility to tweak and amend their social media identity, or even recreate it, until it bears little relation to real life.

Hero Douglas, a teenage musician, said this:

> I don't post photos of me weeping with mascara running down my face after I've fallen out with a friend or screwed up a musical performance. I publish a constant stream of highlights of my life.

63 'Dangerous Curves: Get Thicc, Get Sick?' *BBC Three*, April 2021, bbc.co.uk.

And, of course, my friends put up similar images that illustrate their brilliant lives. It's mostly the highlights we share, not the sad bits when we feel lonely, unattractive, stupid and a failure.[64]

And here lies the danger: a gap develops between real life and our social media identity, and as the gap increases it fuels our anxiety that even if we get lots of 'likes', we won't be able to live up to the 'self' we have created.

Psychologist and author Linda Papadopoulos comments:

> We start to view ourselves in the third person. We effectively step outside ourselves and become observers of our own lives, constantly wondering how we measure up in the eyes of others, ready to edit who we are in order to conform or please.[65]

This pressure was heightened during lockdown. For many teenagers, life lived 24/7 at home would often feel grey and boring compared to the vibrancy and colour of the online world. While hours scrolling through celebrity posts and lockdown highlights of friends' (apparently) more colourful experience of the pandemic may have provided temporary anaesthetic relief to their frustration, it also caused many young people to feel envious and inadequate, dealing a heavy blow to their emerging self-esteem.

After school one Friday evening, 15-year-old Daisy was at her friend's house with some girls from school. She was immature for her age, shy and not as confident as the other more sophisticated and savvy girls. They'd been trying on outfits and taking selfies when one of them suggested they all post their photos on Instagram to see how many 'likes' they'd each get. Daisy's heart sank. She was terrified to take part but even more frightened of not being seen as part of the group, and so, reluctantly, she agreed. It wasn't the best photo of herself, she knew that, but secretly she hoped she'd get a

---

64 Carol Midgley, 'Social media and the trouble with teenage girls', *The Times*, 23 August 2016.
65 Vodafone, 'Digital Parenting', *Vodafone Magazine*, Issue 4, September 2015, vodafone.com.

lot of 'likes' and that this would help her feel more confident with her peers. Later that evening, she plucked up enough courage to check the app. Her heart sank even more as she saw the number. She knew it was stupid, but she couldn't help checking every few minutes, hoping against hope that her total would have increased. She lay awake until the small hours, her thoughts in freefall.

The aptly named 'Life in Likes'[66] report focussed on the effect of social media on 8–12-year-olds, and found that children's wellbeing hit a wall when they started secondary school. At this stage, their use of social media generally changes from games and creativity to focus on social interaction and image. Many children in Years Six and Seven were regularly using image-heavy platforms like Instagram and Snapchat where they could follow adult celebrities. The following comments from the focus groups give us a glimpse into the pressure that many of these children feel:

When you get fifty 'likes', it makes you feel good 'cos you know people think you look good in that photo. Harry, 11

If I got 150 'likes', I'd be like, that's pretty cool, it means they like you. Aaron, 11

I saw a pretty girl and everything she has I want. My aim is to be like her. I want her stuff, her white house and her MAC makeup. Seeing her makes me feel cosy. Birdie, 11

You might compare yourself [to the celebs], 'cos you're not very pretty compared to them. Aimee, 11

An additional pressure now comes in the guise of Instagram influencers. These reality TV stars are paid to promote Instagram accounts of particular brands, including lip filler providers, cosmetic surgery clinics and gambling sites – many of which are unregulated. The Influencers entice their teenage fans to follow these accounts

66 Children's Commissioner, 'Life in "Likes"'.

in return for entry into a prize draw, and the chance to win a 'huge giveaway worth thousands'. Young people who enter the competition may then be flooded with unverified and potentially unsafe links on their Instagram feed. Industry Regulators have called this strategy 'dangerous and irresponsible'. Journalist Celia Walden writing in *The Telegraph* agrees: 'Today's influencers aren't just telling their followers what to do but, with the help of Instagram, are taking them by the hand and showing them the way'.[67]

Hours of unstructured time during lockdown led to many children spending hours on TikTok, watching uploaded videos, and creating their own. It provided an outlet for self-expression, from lip-synch videos to dance crazes, as well as normalizing previously taboo subjects such as body image and mental health.

The powerful algorithm tracks what users interact with and shows them similar content, and with a continuous scroll, it never runs out of material.

Teenager Kayla Christine Long didn't give much thought to posting a video to TikTok on New Year's Eve saying that all she had consumed that day was a jug of ice water. She gave it the hashtag *#whatIeatinaday*. The video amassed an astonishing two million views before she deleted it a week later. The following month, she was diagnosed with an eating disorder. She said that TikTok, along with other influencers on social media like Instagram and Snapchat, had pushed her to restrict her food intake over the past year.

It's a tough world out there for our children, as evidenced by recent statistics on their mental health and wellbeing. Research has found that globally, up to one in five children and teenagers experience a mental health problem each year. In the UK, the NHS reports that one in six (16%) 5–16-year-olds have a mental health difficulty[68] – nearly four in every classroom.

Overall, it's a worrying trend and of course the causes are numerous: academic pressure, family breakdown, worry about

---

67 Celia Walden, 'We Need a Limit on Instagram's Bad Influences', *The Telegraph*, 31 May 2021.
68 NHS, 'Mental Health of Children and Young People in England, 2020', *NHS Digital*, 22 October 2020, digital.nhs.uk.

money and friendship issues; global concerns such as climate change, as well as the impact of COVID-19 are all contributing to an anxious generation.[69] The issues are complex, but it is interesting to note that the rise in anxiety and depression has coincided with the use of the smartphone, and recent research has found, perhaps unsurprisingly, that the more time young people spend on social media the greater the impact on their mental wellbeing.[70] Our brains are highly tuned to social acceptance and rejection, and social media provides fertile soil for anxiety and other negative emotions, particularly among those who are most vulnerable to mental health issues.[71]

The Royal College of Psychiatrists has now said that all young patients should be asked about their screen time and viewing habits amidst growing evidence of links between poor mental health and content seen online. Dr Bernadka Dubicka, Chair of the Child and Adolescent Faculty at the Royal College of Psychiatrists said:

> As a frontline clinician, I regularly see young people who have deliberately hurt themselves after discussing self-harm techniques online. We're also finding that some young people report being recommended harmful content; for example, links to websites encouraging weight loss or displaying self-harm after searching for, or clicking on, similar content once before.[72]

Numbers of children struggling with eating disorders rose dramatically during lockdown, and while not all the blame can lie at the door of social media, experts believe there is a causal link.

Eighteen-year-old Keira, who has suffered from severe depression, self-harming and eating disorders since the age of 13,

69 David Gunnell, Judi Kidger and Hamish Elvidge, 'Adolescent mental health in crisis', *British Medical Journal*, 361, June 2018.
70 Jean M. Twenge, 'More Time on Technology, Less Happiness? Associations Between Digital-Media Use and Psychological Well-Being', *Current Directions in Psychological Science*, vol.28, no.4, 22 May 2019, p372–379.
71 Yvonne Kelly et al., 'Social Media Use and Adolescent Mental Health: Findings From the UK Millennium Cohort Study', *The Lancet*, vol.6, December 2018.
72 'Ask children about social media use, psychiatrists urged', *BBC News*, March 2019, bbc.co.uk.

described the pressures she experienced coming from two directions: exams and social media: 'You're pressured not only into having the looks and weighing a certain amount; it's also [about] getting the perfect grades.'[73] She believes that social media can certainly exacerbate feelings of worthlessness, even if it doesn't actually cause them. 'It's all about how many 'likes' you get.' According to Marjorie Wallace, of the mental health charity Sane:

> One of the problems is the way in which 24/7 exposure on social media can have a potentially destructive effect on issues such as self-esteem, body image or sex. Young people can find themselves damned if they do take part and damned if they don't, as they risk becoming isolated from their peers.[74]

In 2019, there was public outcry when 14-year-old Molly Russell committed suicide after being assailed by graphic self-harm images online. Her father said that Instagram had 'helped to kill' his daughter.

But despite these dangers, social media can be positive and fun, and provided opportunities for creativity, and a lifeline for many during lockdown. Both social media, and the Internet more widely, have been shown to benefit young people with mental health problems because they enable them to communicate with others who are having the same experiences and join online support groups. In an Ofcom study, 90% of 12–15-year-olds said that social media helped them feel closer to their friends.[75] Social media has great benefits for children and young people, but as parents, we need to learn to use it well, and to help our children do the same. In the meantime, its relationship with mental health will continue to be a vital area of research.

73 Carol Midgley, 'Social media and the trouble with teenage girls'.
74 *Ibid.*
75 Ofcom, 'Children and parents: Media use and attitudes report 2018'.

Digital footprint

Whether it's photos, selfies, videos, opinions, or likes and dislikes, many young people see sharing personal information online as a natural extension of their offline lives and the boundaries for each are blurred. As they build their online identity, they will be building a unique 'digital footprint'.

In his first lecture at medical school, a friend's son was warned that future employers may check applicants' social media profile before interview. Rants about animal testing, hunting, climate change, politics or any other issue; pouting poses in changing rooms, videos of high jinks stunts, photos of exam celebrations or drinking games at the sports club dinner ... anything and everything, discreet and indiscreet, will be there (or discoverable) for anyone who wishes to see. It was sobering for these future members of the medical profession to discover that if they weren't careful, the hoped-for string of letters after their names might also come with another less welcome tag.

And what we can see on the screen of our own or other people's identities is just the tip of the iceberg. In completing the 'If you were a dog, what breed would you be?' online quiz, what seems like harmless information may in fact give data-mining companies all kinds of personal information about us that can be stored and enable us to be identified. Google may give us information, but it is not for free: in return, they receive information about us which they can use in a variety of ways. In a recent example, former Children's Commissioner for England Anne Longfield has filed a claim against what she argues is TikTok's excessive data collection policies (a claim TikTok is defending).

COVID restrictions meant we hadn't visited our youngest for the best part of eighteen months and I was excited to be seeing him. After four hours on the motorway, we were glad to finally arrive and sit down with him for a coffee. No sooner had we found an empty table than my husband's phone pinged. It was a notification from the NHS Track and Trace app; he had apparently been near someone who had tested positive for COVID and needed to isolate immediately. The long-awaited reunion was evidently not to be. We returned to the car and began the familiar four-hour journey home. Disappointing as it was to be on the wrong side of the 'ping', this app (and others like it) was a helpful tool for governments monitoring the spread of the pandemic. It is, however, a double-edged sword: while there are some obvious advantages, questions have been raised over issues of surveillance and privacy. Similarly, concerns have been voiced by parents and teachers alike as online classroom apps use cameras which invade the privacy of the family home.

While the power of social media to influence our children's lives might at times feel overwhelming, as parents we can have every confidence that we can be a greater influence on their lives. There is one question on the lips of every child and teenager – in fact, every human being – on planet earth. It's a question that goes to the very heart of human existence: 'Am I loved?'

In a society that screams at our young people, 'I will love you if you are pretty/handsome/slim/clever/popular/good at sports … ', as their parents we have an incredible opportunity to tell them a different story. We have it in our power to build a family where our children know that they are loved not for what they look like and not because of the number of 'likes' or followers they have secured, but simply for who they are. They are being drip-fed the message that image is everything, but we can counter that by showing them that we love them, value them, and accept them as they are.

One of the most effective ways of making a child feel accepted is through what we say. A wise proverb says that our words have 'the power of life',[76] and as parents we can speak life to our children by saying things that will build their confidence and self-esteem. We can do this in the simplest of ways. When my daughter left school, she got a job as a lifeguard at the local gym. The first week didn't go well. The other staff were cliquey and she had to deal with some complaints and some difficult customers. She was on the verge of giving up, and to encourage her I put a note in her bag which simply said, 'Charlotte, we think you're great! ☺'. I thought no more about it; she carried on with the job, went travelling for six months, and

76 The Holy Bible, New International Version, Proverbs 18:21.

then went off to university. About eighteen months later, we were at home and she asked me to grab her bag and get a receipt out of her purse. As I looked for it, I stopped dead in my tracks. There alongside the receipts and lists was that note. She had kept it all that time and even taken it around the world with her. Positive, kind, affirming words can build our children's self-esteem and be literally life-giving.

WHAT PARENTS CAN DO

✓ Find out what it's all about ... and join in

While we don't need to become experts, it is worth finding out about the social media platforms our children are using, if we aren't already familiar with them. Even if we will never be avid users ourselves of our children's app of choice, we can still set up an account so we know how it all works, talk to our children in an informed way, and, if appropriate, engage with them online. (Although one word of caution: your teenagers may not appreciate your Snapchat stories or TikTok dances as much as you do!)

✓ Teach your children the online safety basics

The online safety basics are as key for us to teach our children today as crossing the road, not getting into a car with a stranger, or learning to swim. With younger children, we can talk to them about what they share and explain what 'personal information' is, and why it's important to keep this private. Warn them that not everyone may be who they say they are online, so it's best to speak only to people they know. Rather than giving them a long lecture all at once – which they will probably not take in – have short conversations over a period of time. Help them to choose usernames that don't reveal private information and make sure there are privacy controls on information-sharing apps.

Safety guidelines.
- Avoid sharing your full name in chatrooms or messaging apps.
- Never share your address or telephone number.
- Never tell anyone where you go to school.
- Never agree to meet anyone you meet online on your own. Only meet them in a public place with one of your parents or another adult. If they are genuinely who they say they are, they will be happy to do this.
- Tell an adult if someone makes inappropriate suggestions to you or makes you feel uncomfortable or upset online.

Danger signs.
- If someone tries to insist on getting your address or phone number.
- If someone emails you pictures which make you feel uncomfortable and which you would not want to show to anyone else.
- If someone wants you to email them pictures of yourself or use a webcam in a way which makes you feel uncomfortable.
- If someone wants to keep their chats with you secret and warns you that you'll get in trouble if you tell an adult what has been going on.
- If someone tells you that you will get into trouble if you tell an adult what has been going on.
- If someone wants you to email them pictures of yourself or use a webcam in a way which makes you feel uncomfortable.
- If someone shares information with you and tells you not to tell anyone else about it.
- If someone wants to meet you and tells you not to let anyone know.
- If you come across any of these danger signs it's important that you tell your parents or another adult. (Adapted from advice by Bullying UK.)[77]

77 'How to stay safe online', *Bullying UK*, September 2021, bullying.co.uk.

✓ Put parental controls in place

If young children are in the house, we tend to put things like knives and bleach out of reach. When our children were little, we put the carving knives on a high shelf, and it occurred to me the other day that as our youngest is now 6'3", at 5'1" I am the only person who has to climb on a chair to reach them! In the same way, we can put age-appropriate external safeguards in place to protect our children from digital harm. To do this effectively, we need to be smart, keeping ahead as far as possible – and that means getting informed and taking action.

Parental controls are software tools that you can install on home broadband, phones or tablets, laptops or games consoles to filter the content your child sees when searching online (although this may not always be useful, and can block sites they *do* need to access, for school projects, for example). They will also allow you to set time limits – or use screen time apps – for *when* your child can go online and how long for, and block programmes they are not old enough for. Some companies provide software to filter both computers and phones, which works at home and when out and about.

Some may find this complicated to navigate at first, but it is essential that we don't bury our heads in the sand, leaving our children to their own devices.

There are also privacy controls on social networks that you can make sure are in place. Go to your broadband provider for details about the service they offer and see the appendix for useful sites.

Controls obviously need to be age-appropriate – what is necessary to protect a 10-year-old is likely to be over-restrictive for a 16-year-old – but used wisely, they will go a long way to keeping our children safe.

However, there is a caveat: filters and parental controls are essential, but they will never be 100% effective, and tech-savvy kids are adept at finding a way round them. When our children were young, we were staying for the weekend with some friends from college days. Having got all the children into bed for the night, we settled down with a glass of wine to watch a film, only to discover that their 7-year-old had cracked their password and reset it, blocking parental access. Regaining entry was beyond the competence of his parents, so they had to wake their son up and ask him to do it. I recall that our friends had rather a sense of humour failure on that occasion and didn't find the escapade quite as funny as we did.

✓ Find suitable sites and apps

Don't ignore age guidelines for games, apps and social media – they are there for a reason. See the appendix for organizations which review and recommend sites that are appropriate for children at different ages.

✓ Talk to older children about the long-term effects of everything they do online

If your child is at the younger end of the teen years, you might try sitting down together and looking for them online using different search engines to check their name or nickname, as well as checking Google images. Does anything include private information like their school, address or phone number? How are they representing themselves through photos, 'likes' and comments on social media?

Remind your children that everything they post builds their reputation, and what goes online, stays online. It's important that they use privacy settings on social media and block unwanted contacts, but none of these safeguards are foolproof, and it's difficult to keep things private: accounts can get hacked, and friends can forward photos and messages, or take screen shots on Snapchat. Encourage simple common sense to help them manage personal information and particularly to develop an online reputation that they would be proud of. Research shows that 70% of employers use social media to screen potential employees, and 34% have reprimanded or fired a current employee based on content found online.[78] Perhaps a good test when they are about to post something is to ask themselves: 'Would I want my Granny to see this?', 'Would I want this to be on

78 CareerBuilder, 'More Than Half of Employers Have Found Content on Social Media That Caused Them NOT to Hire a Candidate', *CareerBuilder Survey*, August 2018, press. careerbuilder.com.

'Tag Granny in this photo.
She'd love to see this!'

a poster for my family, friends and the whole school to see?', and 'Would that post take some explaining at a job interview?'

What we do online can also affect others, of course, so talk to them about the old adage 'Do as you would be done by' – or, in other words: be kind. Even if we are not intentionally mean, it can be easy to post something we think is 'funny' at the time, but ends up causing hurt or embarrassment to our friends or family.

✓ Be a good role model

As parents, we can set a good example in the way we use social media, making sure that we never post anything ourselves that we wouldn't want our children to see. For many of us, that may mean taking a good long look at our own social media accounts and seeing how much we 'overshare' – particularly photos of our children. It's worth thinking about the fact that babies today will have a digital footprint from the moment Mummy, Daddy, Auntie or Granddad post online that first photo of them as a new-born. (For more on 'sharenting', see Chapter 17.)

WHEN THINGS GO WRONG

If we discover our children have posted something online that they regret, we can reassure them, listen and tell them that we'll do everything we can to help sort it out. Above all – and as hard as it may be – it's important to try to stay calm. Ask them to tell you exactly what has happened and then, as a first response, help them to delete the post as quickly as possible.

If someone has posted something upsetting or offensive about our child, and they refuse to take it down when asked, we can help report it to the website concerned. It doesn't guarantee that the content will be removed, but the site does have an obligation to do so if it is in breach of their rules. (See appendix for useful websites that can help in this situation.)

CHAPTER 9

PORNOGRAPHY

Our house is next to a little path that goes down to the local school – our four children went to it when they were young. Every morning a procession of mums with buggies, some dads with 2-year-olds on their shoulders and school children in bright blue sweatshirts dragging book bags behind them walk past on the way down to the school. At 3.30pm the procession returns. It all takes me back to when our children were young, and sometimes I feel a sense of sadness that that season is over. But as I've watched these little ones lately, another emotion has overwhelmed me.

I feel angry. Angry that we have sleepwalked into allowing unbelievable dangers to spread into society and threaten children's lives. The fact is that within three or four years, these infants will be able to download hours of pornography with just one tap – because even if they don't have a smartphone themselves, one of their friends will.

After spending six months researching the effects of porn for a TV documentary, ex-lad's mag editor Martin Daubney, now a dad himself, looked back with regret at his involvement with the industry when he was interviewed about the programme:

Internet porn [has] cast its dark shadow over the lives of millions of British teenagers ... I used to be sceptical that porn was as damaging a force as the headlines ... suggest. In the past I'd even defended pornography in university debates, on TV and on radio. I claimed it was our freedom of choice to watch it and said it could actually help add to adult relationships.

But what I saw during the making of the film changed my opinion of pornography forever.

The true stories of boys I met whose lives had been totally taken over by porn not only moved me to tears but also made me incredibly angry that this is happening to our children. And the looks of revulsion on those poor girls' faces in the playground enraged me. I feel as if an entire generation's sexuality has been hijacked by grotesque online porn.[79]

Talking with friends one day, the subject of children and porn came up. Someone said that, statistically speaking, our boys had almost certainly been looking at porn. Later, a friend who had been in the group told me that she'd felt outraged and even slightly insulted – that wouldn't happen in her family. But as she read more about the culture our teens were growing up in, she had a nagging sense that this might be right. She had no evidence – no laptop inadvertently left open next to the maths homework or letters from the school. So she ventured to ask her child directly. She imagined that 'Have you ever seen porn?' might be a naïve approach that would almost certainly be met with a rebuff. Instead, one day in the car, she casually framed the question, 'Just wondering … when did you first see porn?' She wasn't sure what answer she was hoping for. While it wasn't, by then, a surprise (and in case you are wondering, it was during the first year at secondary school at a friend's house), what did surprise her was the nonchalant, matter-of-fact tone in which her son answered. What she'd thought was a big deal, he seemed to take in his stride.

It seems she is not alone, and many of us parents have some catching up to do. I recently met Lucy, a young single mum, at a Care for the Family parenting event. She was crying when she came up to me at the end of the evening. She told me she had three lively boys. Jake was the oldest, and until now he'd been a compliant child who had caused her little concern. But the previous Friday at 7.30 a.m. all that changed when a letter fell onto her doormat from the school. As she read it, her heart missed a beat and her stomach churned; it was from the Head asking her to come to a meeting after school the next day. Some children had been accessing adult porn sites on their smartphones, and it seemed that Jake was in the thick of it.

79 Martin Daubney, 'Experiment that convinced me online porn is the most pernicious threat facing children today', *Daily Mail*, 25 September 2013.

'You look very uncomfortable, Dad.
Is this about sex, porn or drugs?'

The news had sent Lucy spiralling into a state of anxiety. Struggling against the tears, she told me that the initial shock was followed by an overwhelming feeling of shame. What would other parents think? She felt guilty, alone, and didn't know where to begin to deal with the situation. As I listened to her story, my heart went out to her. I told her she wasn't the only parent to receive a letter like that from school, and she wasn't the only parent with a child whose combination of rising hormones and natural curiosity had led them to look at porn. Most of all, I reassured her that as a single mum it wasn't all her fault: the situation was part and parcel of parenting, whatever the shape of the family. The tears subsided and then she hugged me. I hadn't given her clever answers or bright strategies, but I had been able to give her the awareness that she was not alone, and that knowledge had made all the difference to her.

At Care for the Family, we regularly have emails and calls from distraught parents who have made similar discoveries. They feel upset, guilty, and don't know where to go for help.

Kate was cooking the supper and asked Patrick, her husband, to pop upstairs to turn off the light in 9-year-old Joe's bedroom as it was well past his bedtime. At the bedroom door, Patrick could see Joe had made a den under the duvet, and it took him straight back to his own childhood. But when he crept into the room and pulled back the bedclothes to surprise his son, he got more than he bargained for. Young Joe was on his iPad looking at pictures of naked women. Kate was horrified, but Patrick was more philosophical. He remembered the magazines he used to look at in the eighties, which he felt hadn't done him any harm.

While Joe's escapade may have been relatively harmless on that occasion, like many parents, Patrick hadn't grasped an important fact: the material available to our young people today – in both scale and content – is light years away from any magazines he may have looked at in his younger days.

Of course, there's nothing new about pornography, but what is different is that our children are the first generation to have access anywhere and anytime to unregulated free content. Internet enabled smartphones and tablets mean they can now see porn at a speed and on a scale that previously wasn't possible, some of it portraying vicious and violent scenes that can leave an imprint on their lives forever. Like Patrick, many of us are blissfully ignorant of this and of the consequences.

I recently heard a heartbreaking interview with a young man called Matt. He first came across porn at a friend's house after school. Seeing a group of his friends gathered around a laptop, he walked over to find out what was causing such interest. He was amazed at what he saw. In the weeks that followed, he began looking at different porn sites in the privacy of his bedroom and was pleasantly surprised how much he enjoyed the sexual stimulation and release that it gave him. But what began as something he did once in a while began gradually to take a grip on his life and became a habit that he was unable to stop.

In order to satisfy his increasing appetite, he began looking at more explicit and brutal content. At college his porn habit continued … alongside a series of failed relationships with girls. Shortly after college he married, but as a couple they had problems in their sexual relationship. He believed his inability to maintain an erection was a physical problem and went to his GP. The medication he was prescribed only made things worse. He then went to see a counsellor who suggested that he watch porn with his wife to try to overcome his issues – advice they didn't follow. Matt explained what happened after that:

'I was desperate. Eventually I was referred to a therapist who diagnosed 'porn-induced ED' (erectile dysfunction). I couldn't believe what she was saying. She explained that over the years, watching porn had conditioned my brain to be aroused only by seeing sexual images on screens, and it had left me unable to be aroused by my wife. At the time, with all my friends watching porn, it seemed a simple pleasure and I didn't think there was anything wrong with it. It's only now that I understand the

damage it causes. Porn kills intimacy. Young people need to know about this and not have to go through what I have been through.'

Matt has now received the help and support he needed, but his story is not unique. In an interview,[80] Angela Gregory, a psychosexual therapist at Nottingham University Hospital, commented that over the last ten years, she has seen an increasing number of young men presenting with sexual difficulties that have their root in porn and chat room use. Many young people, girls as well as boys, are growing up casually watching porn in the same way they would watch a rom-com or sport on TV. They consider it a 'normal' pastime, not realizing the chemical changes it brings about in the brain, its addictive effect, and the fact that it can ruin their ability to build a healthy sexual relationship.

As a society, we can no longer bury our heads in the sand. Fifty years ago, smoking was an accepted social practice. Unbelievably, advertisements featured doctors promoting cigarettes and pregnant mothers celebrating smoking in pregnancy because it gave the 'win-win' of smaller babies and easy labour. Yet today, cigarettes are locked away in grey cabinets behind the counter, packets come with government health warnings, and smoking is banned in public places because society has realized the damage it causes and has taken action. In the same way, we have been ignorant of the damage that watching pornography can do to our health, especially the health of our children, and again it is time to take action.

As parents, many of us need a wake-up call to understand the seriousness of the issue. If you are still in doubt, here are four reasons why this matters:

1. Porn is addictive. Even if science wasn't your favourite subject at school, it's important to take a moment to understand the effect on the human brain of watching too much porn. We know that pleasurable activity (including watching porn) causes dopamine,

80 Simon Mundie, 'Easy access to online porn is "damaging" men's health, says NHS therapist', *BBC Newsbeat*, August 2016, bbc.co.uk.

the chemical responsible for reward and pleasure, to be released. So the more porn that is watched, the more dopamine is released in this 'reward centre' of the brain.

But here lies the problem. Repeated dopamine surges mean that the brain becomes desensitized to its effects, so after time, a bigger dopamine hit is needed to produce the same feeling. In the same way that, over time, drug users need more drugs to experience a high, so those using porn need more and more stimulation to achieve the same effect.

Dr Jeffery Satinover, a psychiatrist, psychoanalyst, physicist and former fellow in Psychiatry at Yale University, graphically described the addictive effect of pornography to the US Congress:

> It is as though we have devised a form of heroin one hundred times more powerful than before, usable in the privacy of one's own home and injected directly to the brain through the eyes.[81]

Scientists know that watching too much porn can actually rewire the brain. The human brain has an incredible ability to reorganize itself by forming new connections between brain cells as it adapts to new experiences. This ability to change is known as the brain's 'plasticity'. If you become an expert in something new, the area in your brain that deals with this type of skill will actually grow. A study involving London taxi drivers is an interesting example of this as it has shown that they have a larger hippocampus than London bus drivers.[82] This is the part of the brain used for navigation and spatial awareness (which anyone travelling with me can attest is sadly lacking in my case). Bus drivers follow a limited set of defined routes, whereas taxi drivers have to navigate to different destinations from different starting points, and their brains have adapted accordingly.

81 Morgan Bennett, 'The New Narcotic', *Public Discourse*, October 2013, thepublicdiscourse.com.
82 Eleanor A. Maguire, Katherine Woollett and Hugo J. Spiers, 'London Taxi Drivers and Bus Drivers: A Structural MRI and Neuropsychological Analysis', *Hippocampus*, vol.16, 2006, pp1091–1101, ucl.ac.uk.

Over a lifetime, our brains continue to reorganize themselves according to our experiences, and watching porn is no exception. Each time someone looks at porn, dopamine consolidates the new connections made.[83] It is as if a small footpath through a meadow becomes a well-trodden path; the more often it is walked, the more established it becomes, eventually becoming a wide and busy highway. For young people, the effect is even more significant because their brains are more malleable; as we have seen, the prefrontal cortex of the teenage brain is still developing, making them even more vulnerable.

If this sounds all gloom and doom, there is hope! It follows that if the brain is always changing, although it may be difficult, it's never too late to change the pathways by forming new habits. But better still to not get involved in the first place.

2. *Porn gives unrealistic expectations of real relationships.* Porn bombards our young people with images that set wildly unrealistic expectations for real-life relationships. The fundamental problem with porn is that it gives our children the message that sex is a performance which is divorced from relationship, from consent, from respect, from faithfulness and from commitment.

Hardcore videos portray something that has nothing to do with the loving and intimate act of sexual intercourse. Kissing, hugging and tenderness are absent and there is an emphasis on oral sex. Women have surgically enlarged breasts, men have penis enlargements, pubic hair is non-existent, and girls who don't go along with the trend for porn-inspired waxing are considered 'ugly' and 'gross'.

The images of tiny waists and Kardashian bums put an incredible pressure on girls to act and look a particular way (well-nigh impossible for even the most shapely among us). Sixteen-year-old Marna said, 'The pressure on us is massive. I know I can't compete, but it doesn't stop me feeling that I have to.' These images also do our boys no favours by giving them unrealistic expectations of women and sex.

83 Gary Wilson, *Your Brain on Porn: Internet Pornography and the Emerging Science of Addiction,* (Commonwealth Publishing, 2015).

And it's not just confined to what they see, but what they hear; some of the language used is brutal. As author Allison Havey put it:

> It's not only the images. The language on pornographic sites is very particular too: verbs such as 'nailed', 'hammered', 'screwed', 'pummelled'. Anyone would think it was an advert for a DIY store.[84]

You may or may not be surprised to hear that many teens believe that the best way to learn about sex is to view porn. Author Peggy Orenstein writes:

> Kids look at porn, in part, as an instruction manual, even though it's about as realistic as pro wrestling … Girls would ask me all the time, 'My boyfriend wants to know why I don't make all those noises like porn stars during sex,' and I would say, 'Because [porn] is a movie.'[85]

But real life is not a movie. And here is the irony. A healthy sexual relationship is the culmination of the closest, most loving, tender and intimate connection possible between two real people. But porn has exploited sex in such a way that it has become an impersonal solitary act of masturbation while watching fantasy images. Our teenagers have been sold a counterfeit – and many have no idea.

3. Porn is changing. Whereas when we were growing up, pornography was primarily found in photographs and film, now it is evolving and becoming more interactive. One particularly alarming trend is an increase in 'self-generated' pornography among children. In some cases, children – often girls - are coerced or tricked into producing and sharing sexual images or videos of themselves, sometimes in their own room via their webcam. A representative from the Internet Watch Foundation reported that this type of activity is often

84 Joanna Moorhead, 'How porn is damaging our children's future sex lives', *The Guardian*, September 2016.
85 Peggy Orenstein, *Girls and Sex: Navigating the Complicated New Landscape*, (Harper, 2016).

going on in a household setting when parents are present: 'There are conversations that you can hear [in the background], even children being asked to come down for tea.'[86] This material is then published online. There are online communities of adults which are focussed on getting hold of self-generated images. In fact, one study found that 44% of all online child sexual abuse content involved this type of material.[87]

Sadly, as technology develops, it is likely that other similarly interactive forms of child sexual exploitation will emerge. As parents, while we don't want to assume that every person our child communicates with online is intending to groom them to take photos of themselves, we must be aware that this is happening, and keep the lines of communication open about what they're doing online.

4. *Porn is becoming 'normal'.* Porn is everywhere. In fact, back in 2011 one review already described sexualized culture as 'the "wallpaper" of children's lives'.[88] A Headteacher who tried to do something about porn in her school was told by parents as well as pupils that she was old-fashioned and that 'everyone does it'.[89] And an American study found that 56% of young people considered it wrong to not recycle (which, of course, is a good thing), but only 32% of the same children thought viewing porn was wrong.[90]

If you like stats, here are some sobering ones to think about:

- More than half (51%) of 11–13-year-olds reported having seen online porn at some point.

86 IWF, 'Face the Facts', *Internet Watch Foundation Annual Report*, 2020, iwf.org.uk.
87 *Ibid.*
88 Reg Bailey, 'Letting Children Be Children: Report of an Independent Review of the Commercialisation and Sexualisation of Childhood', *Department for Education*, 2011, gov.uk.
89 Barbara McMahon, 'Teenage girls and sex: do you really know what's going on?', *The Times*, 28 May 2016.
90 British Board of Film Classification, 'Children see pornography as young as seven, new report finds', *BBFC Research into children and pornography 2019*, 2020, bbfc.co.uk.

- Two thirds (66%) of 14–15-year-olds have seen porn and the first exposure to it is often accidental: 62% 11–13-year-olds said this was the case.
- Seventy-five per cent of parents thought their child hadn't watched online porn, but 53% of their children reported that they had.
- Substantial minorities of older children (42% of 15–16-year-olds) wanted to try things out they had seen in pornography.[91]

Even if our young people don't actively look for porn, it may well find them. (I recently heard of a mum whose son was doing a project on the City of London and got more than he bargained for after innocently typing 'Big Ben' in the search engine.) Remembering the day she discovered her daughter had been secretly watching hardcore pornographic videos with friends, after being introduced to the videos by another child, is still upsetting for another mum:

> She's 8 … She still believes in Santa Claus and the Tooth Fairy. You think you are doing everything right and then you discover you've been invaded by an intrusive, outside, evil scummy force. It's so gut-wrenching. The sadness of an innocence lost. You only get one childhood.[92]

According to a 2020 survey, the average age of first exposure to porn is 13 years old, with the youngest exposure as early as 7.[93]

Many mainstream music videos watched by children (check out Ariana Grande, Dua Lipa or Little Mix just for starters) are, arguably, inches from porn. This indirect messaging has the effect of making porn or near-porn a 'normal' part of life for our children.

91 Sara Israelsen-Hartley, 'How to talk to your kids about porn', *Deseret News*, 14 August 2014, deseret.com.
92 British Board of Film Classification, 'Children see pornography as young as seven, new report finds'.
93 British Board of Film Classification, 'Young people, pornography & age verification', *BBFC Research into children and pornography 2019*, 2020, bbfc.co.uk.

All this is not intended to be alarmist or to engender a sense of panic, but to open our eyes to the issues and, in doing so, equip us to protect our children from the dangers of porn and prevent them becoming its victims. Let's not walk blindly into a society where 'porn is the norm' for our children.

WHAT PARENTS CAN DO

✓ Talk about it

At home, we can set up every possible external protection there is, but the same filters may not be in place on public Wi-Fi. And of course, there may well be no controls at all at a friend's house or on a friend's device. So as well as using filters and controls in our homes, we must also equip our children to operate their own controls – to self-regulate. This means that we need to be talking to them positively about sex, about relationships, about faithfulness and, in this context, the issue of porn. There is no room for us to feel embarrassed about this or even worried that if we talk about porn it will fuel their curiosity. All children are sexual beings and are going to be curious about sex ... so it's a lot better to instil values in our children before the porn industry gets to them.

A report commissioned by the NSPCC and the Children's Commissioner found that teenagers wanted to find out about sex and relationships in ways that were 'safe, private and credible'.[94] Ed Brook, who works with the national sexual health service for under-25s, said in an interview with *The Times* that 'Year 10 school surveys "overwhelmingly" reveal that teens want mum or dad, more than peers or teachers, to talk about sex. They want to hear it from their parents.'[95] Who better fits the bill? As their parents, we are the most significant influence in their lives ... and yet 75% of parents avoid

---

94 Elena Martellozzo, et al.,'"I wasn't sure it was normal to watch it": The impact of online pornography on the values, attitudes, beliefs and behaviours of children,' *NSPCC/OCC/Middlesex University*, May 2017, childrenscommissioner.gov.uk.
95 Barbara McMahon, 'Teenage girls and sex: do you really know what's going on?'.

discussing porn with their teens.[96]

Cindy Gallop, an Oxford graduate who founded the website www.makelovenotporn.com said, 'We're at a zeitgeist moment. You cannot avoid your children seeing porn. If parents want their child to be happy, they have to tackle it.'[97]

As their children had grown up, Tim and Jade had talked to them about the facts of life but had never mentioned porn. They knew it was an issue they needed to address at some point, but it felt awkward and alien territory, and they had no idea how to begin. They agreed that Tim would talk to the boys and Jade to the girls. Tim put it off for ages, and then one day at work he read an article about the effect of porn on children and realized he couldn't procrastinate any longer. Sitting round the kitchen table that evening, he awkwardly blurted out that he'd read an article that he wanted to talk to them about. He admitted that he was clumsy and slightly embarrassed and didn't make a great job of it, but said that having the conversation wasn't as bad as he'd feared. He realized that his children knew more than he did, and in hindsight his main regret was that he hadn't done it five years earlier.

And in these discussions, we have to do better than just saying, 'Don't watch porn.' Talking to our children about sex can feel embarrassing, but embarrassment is a luxury we can't afford. If we don't talk to them, they may well get unhelpful information about sex from friends or, worse still, from viewing porn.

We found over the years that our children generally didn't respond well to the 'big talk' or lecture; it usually resulted in embarrassment on both sides and a sigh of relief once it was over. Better was the 'little and often' approach; fostering a continuing open and honest conversation, planting seeds, perhaps commenting on the values behind adverts, articles or programmes, listening to their point of view, and explaining to them that porn is as far removed from the reality of real sex as films are to real life.

---

96 Allison Havey and Deana Puccio, *Sex, Likes and Social Media: Talking to Our Teens in the Digital Age* (Vermillion, 2016), p95.
97 Barbara McMahon, 'Teenage girls and sex: do you really know what's going on?'.

✓ Start when they are young

When toddlers ask where the baby guinea pig came from we can begin a conversation in preparation for the more challenging questions that will no doubt follow hard on its heels! At our Care for the Family events we often say to parents, 'When it comes to your own children, nobody knows your child like you and nobody loves your child like you. Have confidence in your parenting.' In the same way, as parents we must have confidence in talking to our children about sex and relationships – there is nobody better placed than us. Schools can do a great job teaching about sex, but they only convey the facts. As parents, we can talk to our children about sex in the context of relationships and our values, remembering to keep it simple, age appropriate and positive. Above all, let them know they can always talk to us if they see anything that frightens, confuses or upsets them, and that they won't be in trouble.

There are some useful resources we can use to help our children which are listed in the appendix. For younger children the NSPCC's friendly singing and dancing, pants-wearing dinosaur, Pantosaurus, helps start simple conversations. This includes teaching children the acronym PANTS: Privates are private; Always remember your body belongs to you; No means no; Talk about secrets that upset you; Speak up, someone can help.

And the Naked Truth Project suggests teaching children the Three Ts: Turn away; Turn it off; and Tell a trusted adult. It also suggests telling them that 'talking about it is always best, no matter how bad it seems'.

For older teenagers a YouTube animation uploaded by Thames Valley Police brilliantly uses different scenarios of people offering each other a cup of tea to address the issue of consenting sex.[98] One mum recently told me she had watched the clip with her daughter and that it had resulted in a great conversation about sex, faithfulness and marriage, and had empowered her daughter to have the confidence to say 'no'.

---

98 Thames Valley Police, 'Tea and Consent', *Consent is Everything*, 2016, thamesvalley. police.uk.

WHEN THINGS GO WRONG

If you discover that your child has been accessing porn or that porn is an issue for them, it's important to be there for them and point them in the direction of any help they need. Showing our child unconditional love and acceptance (see Chapter 8) at a time like this may be very hard for many parents. We first have to cope with our own emotions, perhaps anger as well as dismay, hurt, guilt, and confusion as to how this has come about. But compassionate love and understanding for our child is vital to dealing well with this issue. Realize that they are likely to be suffering from extreme shame and embarrassment, so help them feel safe enough to be open with you about the full story.

While there is no room for complacency, don't let the prospect of porn and the digital age overwhelm you: although porn is pervasive, not all young people have seen it. And of those who have, it certainly doesn't mean they will become addicted. Putting the safeguards in place, beginning open and honest conversations from early childhood and, most importantly, giving them real-life positive examples of healthy relationships will put them in the best possible place for withstanding the pressures of growing up in a sexualized society and digital age.

CHAPTER 10

SEXTING

I was educated at an all-girls school, and I still remember the excitement one day in assembly when it was announced that we would be putting on a play in partnership with the local boys' school. Never before had so many girls wanted a career on the stage. Hoping for the lead role (Joan of Arc), I went along to the auditions and ended up being cast as the executioner. It was at the first rehearsal that I met Ian, and when it finished he passed me a note asking if we could meet up. I was flattered and excited, and I returned the favour. And so our (short-lived!) relationship began. Flirting, dating and taking a romantic interest in peers is all part of growing up, but instead of scruffy notes passed hastily during art lessons, the process is now conducted by text or online messages. And, for our teenagers today, this can involve photos and images, often of a sexual nature.

Sexting is when someone sends sexually explicit texts, or naked or semi-naked photos or videos (of themselves or others) using a mobile or other device. Many young people see this as flirting; some even view it as a necessary precursor to starting a relationship. Sending a revealing selfie can make someone feel good about themselves and may be seen as harmless fun. Boys may ask for a picture of a girl in a skimpy top, topless, or even naked to see if they pass muster before asking them out on a date. And many girls, not wanting to offend, feel under immense pressure to agree. One 15-year-old said, 'My boyfriend asked for a topless selfie and I thought that if I didn't send it he wouldn't like me.' And it's not just girls; boys also may feel under pressure to send pictures of themselves – in a macho pose, topless to show off a six-pack gym body, or even naked.

In an article on the issue, *The Times* reported:

> Britain is suffering from a sexting crisis with tens of thousands of schoolchildren caught sharing sexual imagery online in the past three years … Data from 50 of Britain's biggest secondary schools showed that more than a third of all sexting cases involved children aged 12 and 13.[99]

Commenting on the data, an NSPCC spokesman said that the situation was particularly worrying because in one in ten cases these pictures were sent to adults: 'Sexting can make young people targets for sex offenders or set them up for bullying by their peers.'[100] A survey of 3,000 young people in 2018 revealed that:

- Thirteen per cent of secondary school students have sent a naked photo or video of themselves.
- The rate increased with age: 34% of sixth formers said they had.
- Boys were twice as likely (17%) to sext than girls (9%).[101]

A recent report from *The Guardian* also revealed some shocking statistics: more than 6,000 children under 14 have been investigated by police for sexting offences in the past three years, including more than 300 of primary school age. Figures disclosed by twenty-seven police forces in England and Wales revealed 306 cases of children under 10, including some as young as 4, being investigated on suspicion of taking or sharing indecent images of themselves or other minors since 2017. In one case, a 9-year-old boy was recorded on a police database for sending a naked selfie to a girl on Facebook Messenger.[102]

---

99 Alexi Mostrous and Elizabeth Rigby, 'Schools hit by sexting epidemic', *The Times*, 12 March 2016.
100 *Ibid.*
101 RTE, 'Older teens more likely to "sext" – survey', *RTE Newsroom*, January 2018, rte.ie.
102 Josh Halliday, 'Thousands of children under 14 have been investigated by the police for sexting,' *The Guardian*, 30 December 2019.

We have already seen that in adolescence the prefrontal cortex of the brain, which plays an important part in problem-solving and impulse control, isn't fully formed. This means that risks and consequences are not properly weighed up – the brakes are not yet in place – and, of course, this can come at a cost. What may start off as a private message can be shared (and even manipulated) by others in a matter of seconds. According to one child protection expert, nearly half of all schoolgirls have regretted sending images via Instagram and Snapchat, and the NSPCC has reported that Childline counselling sessions about sexting are on the increase.[103]

Sharing sexually explicit material without consent in order to cause embarrassment and harm ('revenge porn') is another issue we should be aware of as parents. Leo and Chloe are both 16. They began dating and sent intimate texts to each other which gradually became more sexual in nature. This was followed by photos and then videos. At a party one evening, Leo saw Chloe with another boy and to get his own back he decided to post a nude picture of her on Instagram. Before she was aware of what had happened, the image had been shared among all their friends. Chloe, ashamed and embarrassed, was devastated. The picture was taken down fairly quickly, but the damage had already been done. (It is illegal to disclose a private sexual photograph or film without the consent of the person depicted in the content and with the intent to cause them distress.)[104]

A friend's son recently had a very sobering experience. He began a conversation online with someone he didn't know, but whom he believed to be a girl his own age. Over the weeks that followed she encouraged him to send increasingly sexually explicit images to her on Snapchat, and then one day he received a blackmail threat: if he didn't send money, she would post the images publicly on Instagram. This lad went into an utter panic. He shut down the account and after a few anxious and sleepless nights told his mother, who was able to offer him support and advice. Fortunately for him,

103 Holly Bentley, et al., 'How Safe Are Our Children? The most comprehensive overview of child protection in the UK', *NSPCC*, September 2018, learning.nspcc.org.uk.
104 Sexual Offences Act, 2003, legislation.gov.uk.

the threats were not carried out, but it could so easily have resulted in actions that would have scarred him and his reputation for life.

A couple of things to bear in mind about sexting:

1. It's illegal for under-18s. Many parents (and children!) may be surprised to know that it is illegal in the UK to take, hold or share indecent pictures of anyone under 18. So even though the legal age of consent for sexual intercourse is 16, the legal age to send a sexually explicit photo is 18.[105] If under-18s take a nude photo and share it (even with friends of the same age) they are breaking the law. (Whether the police take action is another matter, but the law is there for their protection.)

2. What goes online, stays online. Once you've hit 'send', you have lost control of that picture. While apps such as Snapchat promise to automatically delete your 'snap' after ten seconds, this can't be relied upon as a means of ensuring it is still under your control. The recipient could take a screen shot and then pass it on, and there are many other ways in which the photo can be shared and misused by others. There really is no 'delete' button.

WHAT PARENTS CAN DO

✓ Talk about it

The results of a YouGov poll asking parents what issues affecting their children they were concerned about, showed that more were worried about sexting than they were about smoking or drinking.[106] Despite this concern, however, the NSPCC comments that most parents have a 'worrying level of ignorance' about the issue.[107]

Along with so many other areas, a key strategy for us as parents is to have conversations as early as possible with our children, not

---

105 *Ibid.*
106 PSHE, 'Parents call for education to address sexting by children and young people', *PSHE Association*, July 2016, pshe-association.org.uk.
107 Sian Griffiths, 'Parents too shy to tackle sexting', *The Times*, 14 August 2016.

to wait until it happens. In the same way as we need to talk to them about porn, we can talk to our children about sexting, healthy relationships, and why they might want to send the picture in the first place.

Childline's 'Zipit' is a great app that helps children 'get flirty chat back on the right track' with tips on how to keep control, and clever comebacks to download and send if they are asked to send a naked photo. There are lots to choose from including a picture of a tortoise with the caption, 'Slow Down', a supermarket trolley and the caption, 'Don't push too far', and even a ram with the caption, 'Horny? Not my problem'. And a good video to watch with them is *Exposed* by the Child Exploitation and Online Protection Centre which shows what can potentially happen as a result of sharing images.

✓ Encourage your children to 'think twice'

Help them weigh up the consequences carefully, and encourage them to *think, think* and then *think* again before they post something. When the government is drafting legislation on matters of national security, it often includes what is known as a 'double lock' – checks and balances to go through before action can be taken. Encourage your teens to have a 'double lock' in place – a mental checklist of things to consider before they post a photo and particularly before sharing another person's image. Ask them open questions to help them reflect: how will it stay private? How can you stop it being passed on? If it was passed on, who might see it? How would that make you feel? How would that make them feel? A good test is to ask, 'Would you do this offline? Would you really stand topless in front of your geography class or ask your friend to stand naked outside McDonalds?' Remind them that doing these things online is no different.

WHEN THINGS GO WRONG

A couple I met with recently told me how their daughter had come to them in great distress. She had sent a topless selfie to her boyfriend, which had subsequently been uploaded to social media without any privacy controls. The photo had spread like wildfire – all her friends and classmates had seen it. Their daughter was humiliated and inconsolable. She couldn't face her friends and didn't want to go to school. Her mum and dad had no idea what to do. They were completely wrong-footed by what had happened and were struggling to manage their own feelings of anger and shame, while knowing they needed to be there for their daughter. We chatted through the situation, and a few weeks later I received an email from them:

> *'Thank you so much for listening. We just needed somewhere to 'vent' as we knew being mad with her wouldn't help anyone. The school has been brilliant, and we have managed to get the photos taken down. It's been such a lesson for all of us.'*

If you find your child has sent a selfie that they regret, stay calm (sometimes easier said than done), reassure them and help them deal with the consequences. They may be worried and embarrassed, so remind them that we all make mistakes and that, as hard as it may be, you will help them see the situation through. Try to find out as much about the context as possible, in particular why they sent it, and ask them who the photo has been sent to and where it has been shared.

Help them to delete the photo or photos from their phone and online accounts, but keep copies of the evidence in case you need it. If possible, see if they can contact the person the image was sent to and ask them to delete it as well.

When sexting messages are shared on social media or other sites you can report it with your child and ask the service providers or website to take the image down. Inform your child's school about what has happened and ask for their help both in controlling the circulation and supporting your child. If the image has been shared by one of their pupils, the school can help you approach them directly. If it is more serious and you think your child has been coerced into sending an image, or if it has been shared with an adult, you may need to get in contact with the police. See appendix for more information.

A Pew Research Center report seems to have summed up the current situation well:

> The desire for risk-taking and sexual exploration during the teenage years, combined with a constant connection via mobile devices, creates a 'perfect storm' for sexting ... [Teenagers'] coming-of-age mistakes and transgressions have never been so easily transmitted and archived for others to see.[108]

It's time to take action before the storm heads our family's way – and as parents we are in the very best place to do this.

108 Amanda Lenhart et al., 'Teens and Mobile Phones', *Pew Research Center*, April 2010, pewinternet.org.

CHAPTER 11

ONLINE BULLYING

'Night, love! Sleep tight. Don't let the bedbugs bite.' Crystal paused on the stairs. Her mum said the same thing every night. It got on her nerves a bit – though she admitted to herself that she'd probably miss it if Mum suddenly didn't say it. It was 10.30pm and her heart was hammering. As she opened her bedroom door, she felt sick. She undressed slowly and climbed under the duvet. Her comfy mattress felt like stone. The minutes ticked by and she stiffened – waiting. Perhaps tonight would be different …

But then it came: the familiar beep from the depths of her school bag. She'd left her phone there deliberately, rather than putting it on her bedside table, a visible threat. She screwed her eyes tight and desperately tried to sleep, but after some minutes the beep came again. It was impossible to ignore. She crawled out of bed, her stomach cramping. Unearthing her phone from her bag, she clicked onto the message. It was, of course, from one of her tormentors. Since escaping them at the end of school, she'd seen the comments online, but in the last couple of hours there had been silence. She'd known it would be short-lived. Her phone beeped again. She read the text and stuffed the phone under her pillow. She waited, her eyes open in the dark.

For children today there is no escape from the school bully at the end of the day. They are there on the bus and during the walk home; they lurk as homework is done and the evening meal is eaten; they force their way into the bedroom at night. There is no safe haven. The bully can reach their prey at anytime and anywhere.

The scale and the speed of digital communication also means that what starts off as an unkind joke or two can quickly spiral out of control into abuse. Comments about weight, body shape, clothes, glasses, hair colour, skin, lack of sporting ability or any other number of issues are all there to be viewed by and passed on to others further and further afield.

A friend told me about her 13-year-old niece, Emma. Emma seems to have hit puberty a little bit ahead of her peers and was already suffering with some unwelcome teenage spots. Her 'friends' counted up the number of spots on her Snapchat profile photo, and then 'shared' it with the spots highlighted. What does that kind of experience do for a child's self-esteem?

And unkind messaging isn't limited to teenagers. The *Today* programme on Radio 4 discussed online safety and featured an interview with Matteo who is in Year Five. Matteo plays a game online where one person has to draw something while the other person guesses what it is. 'They couldn't guess what I drew, and then someone called me an a-hole. I felt really upset so I straight away told my mum,' he told Victoria Derbyshire. Matteo's mum said she blocked that person but could do 'absolutely nothing' about it. 'I feel extremely guilty that he had had access to that.'[109]

While some children will take the odd joke or insult in their stride, if bullying is repeated and abusive, it can have a devastating effect on their mental health. Schoolwork can suffer, and some may resort to coping mechanisms which lead to self-harming, eating disorders, drug or alcohol abuse.[110]

Online bullying is when the perpetrator uses social media and messages on the Internet to bully another person, usually repeatedly. Matters are made worse still because abusive and humiliating messages and images can be shared, which means that they are seen by more people and for a longer period than any other kinds of bullying. And it's more common than many of us would think. In 2020, one in five children aged 10–15 experienced some form of online bullying; a quarter of them did not report it to anyone.[111] And in a survey of 1,500 13–18-year-olds, a quarter reported that they were singled out for abuse 'all or most of the time'.[112] Increased

109 'Online safety: Internet "not designed for children"', *BBC News*, 5 January 2017, bbc.co.uk.
110 Dr Hayley van Zwanenberg, 'Analysis: Impulsive act that can easily ruin a young life', *The Times*, 12 March 2016.
111 Nick Stripe, 'Online bullying in England and Wales: year ending March 2020', *Office for National Statistics*, November 2020, ons.gov.uk.
112 Safer Internet, 'Creating a better internet for all', *UK Safer Internet Centre*, February 2016, saferinternet.org.uk.

parental concern about online bullying became a reality for many vulnerable children during the pandemic; nearly a quarter of parents reported that their child experienced it, an increase of 21% since January 2020.[113]

Online bullying can be carried out in a number of ways. These include:

- Sending hurtful, nasty texts and emails.
- Sharing someone's personal information or images without their permission.
- Posting a humiliating video of someone on sites such as YouTube, including 'happy slapping' – videos of personal attacks.
- Setting up profiles that make fun of someone on social media.
- Deliberately sending someone viruses to damage their computer.
- Making abusive comments about another player on a gaming site.

The most common impact on children of online bullying is on their confidence, self-esteem and mental and emotional wellbeing. Most young people think it's as harmful as other forms of bullying and some consider it worse because the abuse is 'permanent' in the form of an online record which can be shared with many people very quickly and cannot be deleted.[114]

Common responses from those who are being bullied are loss of appetite, poor sleep, anxiety, withdrawal, missing school and stopping socializing. Children and young people who have experienced cyberbullying are more than twice as likely to enact self-harm or suicidal behaviour, according to a study.[115] Sadly there

113 Internet Matters, 'From Survive to Thrive: supporting digital family life after lockdown'.
114 Vodafone, 'Groundbreaking Vodafone global survey results on teen cyberbullying', *Vodafone Group Media Relations*, 22 September 2015, vodafone.com.
115 Ann John et al., 'Self-Harm, Suicidal Behaviours, and Cyberbullying in Children and Young People: Systematic Review', *Journal of Medical Internet Research*, vol.20, no.4, April 2018, jmir.org.

have been some high-profile cases of victims of bullying being driven to suicide. After years of relentless bullying in school and on social media, 17-year-old Felix Alexander took his own life in April 2016. His mother, Lucy, said that the bullying had begun with unkindness and social isolation and then, with the advent of social media, over the years it had become cruel and overwhelming.[116]

The Netflix drama *13 Reasons Why* centres around a teenage girl who commits suicide, leaving behind thirteen tapes explaining the reasons that drove her to take her own life. Each episode reveals the next tape in the unfolding drama. While the series was praised for highlighting issues such as bullying, it also received criticism for glamorizing suicide and encouraging copycat deaths among young teens who could be watching alone on a smartphone in their bedroom. In the end, Netflix chose to edit out the lengthy suicide scene from Season One of the series.[117]

On a visit to family friends, I found myself chatting to their teenage daughter who had recently started secondary school. I have known her since she was a toddler. At family gatherings she was always the life and soul of the party, but as I watched her mindlessly scrolling on her phone it felt as if something had changed. She had lost that zest for life. She was wearing a cardigan even though it was a hot day, and as it slipped off her shoulder, I couldn't help noticing the scars at the top of her arm. Her mum caught my eye and quickly looked away again. Later that day we had a chance to chat. She had not coped well with the transition to secondary school; her new friends had encouraged her to join an anonymous chat room, where she had been the butt of unkind humour. She was stressed about her friendships and schoolwork, and had become increasingly anxious about her appearance. While she would say that social media was her lifeline, her mother also knew that it was on Instagram that she had first been exposed to sites with the hashtag, #self-harm.

---

116 Nicola Slawson, 'Mother of teenager who killed himself appeals for kindness online', *The Guardian*, 5 October 2016.
117 '13 Reasons Why: Netflix removes suicide scene from season one', *BBC News*, 16 July 2019, bbc.co.uk.

WHAT PARENTS CAN DO

✓ Watch out for signs that your child may be experiencing online bullying

- A sudden change in the amount of time they are on their phone or computer – either more or less – might signal a possible problem. (But remember that a child's interest will ebb and flow, so it will all depend on the context.)
- Suddenly having lots of new contacts on their social media account – they may not all be 'friends'.
- Changes in their mood when they are on social media. Watch out for how they seem when they put their phone away or close their laptop, particularly if they are nervous or jumpy.
- Asking you how they can block others on, or delete, their social media account (or finding out that they have done this).
- Eating and sleeping problems, or unexplained physical symptoms such as headaches or stomach upsets.
- Negative statements about themselves, others or life in general and any indications of a dip in self-esteem, for example, head held low.

Do remember that the last two warning signs may be indications of problems with completely different causes, so these alone do not mean that your child is being cyberbullied.

✓ Give your child your support

When our daughter was having a particularly difficult time with a friendship group at school, and messages and social media posts were flying about, my advice to her was, 'Just ignore it'. She has since told me how unhelpful that recommendation was (zero out of ten there for my parenting skills). Rather too late in the day, my daughter (now a young adult) tells me a much better approach would have been to have listened to her (instead of jumping in with my timely advice) and reassured her that the bullying wasn't her fault. It can be really upsetting as a parent to hear about, but do your best to remain calm and let your child know that you will help them through it.

✓ Don't stop your child going online
If children are the butt of unkind jokes or the victims of bullying, it will be almost impossible for them to 'just ignore it' and telling them not to go online or stopping them using their devices is also likely to be counterproductive. We might as well be asking them not to breathe, and it would most probably lead to them feeling more isolated and cut off from any network of friends that they do have.

✓ Tell your child not to reply
All bullies are looking for a reaction, so advise your child not to reply or retaliate in any way. If an online conversation becomes abusive or makes them feel uncomfortable, they should simply leave it.

✓ Block messages
Tell your child to block the sender and report them to their social media network or the gaming platform.

✓ Get outside support
Talk to your friends to get support for yourself, and, if necessary, go to your child's school as they should have an anti-bullying policy. In extreme cases, and especially if you feel your child is in danger, consider informing the police. Think also about whether to get outside help for your child. Counselling may be of benefit both during and after the episode.

✓ Be aware of self-harm
If you are concerned that your child might be self-harming, there is a lot of help available. Your GP will be able to advise and can make a referral to NHS Child and Adolescent Mental Health Services. www. youngminds.org.uk is an excellent website primarily for teenagers and children. It is full of resources and includes numbers to text or call for help.

WHAT PARENTS CAN DO: WHEN OUR CHILD IS THE BULLY

As unwelcome as the thought is, as parents we may have to face up to the fact that our child is joining in with bullies by acquiescing in an unkind campaign or even that they are the main perpetrator. It's easy to be defensive about our children, but it's important to find out the full story. If our child is bullying online, we won't be helping them (or their victim) by denying it. If this happens, it's important to remember that we all say things we don't mean at times, and rather than jumping in too hastily, we need to try to discover what is really going on.

There are a number of different motives for online bullying, sometimes it is done out of anger, frustration or to get revenge; sometimes it is done simply out of boredom and for entertainment – to get laughs or a reaction. Some children do it to make themselves feel more powerful, tormenting others to boost their ego. And then there are those who think they are righting wrongs – perhaps standing up for someone else or taking a stand against an issue they see as unjust. Finally, there are those who have simply bullied almost by accident – not thinking through what they are doing or not realising the impact it will have. One of the deterrents to face-to-face bullying is that the perpetrator is made aware that the recipient is a real person with real feelings. With online bullying the contact is less personal because it is all done via a screen and may be even harder to combat.

✓ Talk it through

As upset as we might feel, it's important to stay calm and talk things through. In the same way as if they were involved in sexting, ask your children open questions and try to help them understand the effect of their actions on the other person's feelings. Without face-to-face connection, it can be easy for comments to be misinterpreted or misunderstood, so emphasize the importance of thinking through what they post online. Something that initially seems funny might easily end up causing great harm.

Childline's section on cyberbullying has some great age-appropriate resources that your child can go through with you or by themselves (see the appendix).

✓ Don't condone it

There may be factors that help to explain your child's behaviour, but while taking these into account, it's important not to blame someone else. Show your child that taking responsibility for their own actions is the right thing to do. If they were bullying online in retaliation to being bullied themselves (or on another child's behalf), tell them that two wrongs don't make a right and will just encourage the bully's behaviour. If appropriate, help them face up to their actions and, as hard as it may be to do, apologize to the person concerned.

✓ Don't confiscate their devices

You may want to limit their online access, but this could make the situation worse and encourage them to find other ways to get online.

✓ Try to find out the reasons

Remember that the old saying 'hurting people hurt people' has a lot of truth in it, so take time to see if there is anything going on in your child's life that has made them act in this way. Think about whether there is anything that may be upsetting or angering them and leading them to express these feelings online.

CHAPTER 12

GROOMING

Kayleigh was 15 when she received a friend request on Snapchat from another girl:

> 'She was very friendly – we began chatting and we found we had lots in common. After a few weeks, she asked me to send her a topless photo of myself. I didn't reply, but she kept on asking. I was really worried and didn't know what to do, but ended up telling my mum. The police eventually got involved. They contacted Snapchat and discovered that the message had in fact come from a man who was older than my dad.'

It seems that every day there is another story about online grooming. It's an issue to strike terror into the heart of any parent, and while the purpose of this book is not to scaremonger, sadly it is something that we cannot ignore. The groomer's method is all about befriending and building an emotional relationship with a child, gaining their trust in order to take advantage of them sexually. The Child Exploitation and Online Protection Centre (CEOP) reports that 13–14-year-olds represent the largest single victim group.[118] This may include the groomer having sexual conversations with them online or by text message, getting them to send images or videos of themselves naked, doing something sexually explicit on webcam or meeting up with them in person. Grooming also takes place face to face of course, but the anonymity of digital communication means there is huge scope for the predator. In fact, according to the CEOP, most offences of grooming now take place online.

---

118 'What is child sexual exploitation?', *The Children's Society*, 2021, childrenssociety.org.uk.

During the pandemic, parents reported a large increase in livestreaming on platforms such as YouTube Live or Facebook Live. There was a 43% increase in children watching live broadcasts and an 89% increase in actively broadcasting their own videos.[119] Undoubtedly, this gave a positive opportunity for creativity, connection with large groups of friends and the chance to mirror their online heroes. However, more streaming also led to increased use of chatrooms and forums, and therefore more possibilities for children to chat to people they didn't know, and to share or be exposed to inappropriate content.

Groomers may not always be strangers; in some cases they may have met the children socially and use the Internet to build a relationship with them. They may be male or female, old or young and generally use a false identity with fake profile pictures, building the relationship gradually by pretending to share mutual interests and experiences. Often they join social networks used by young people and pretend to be one of them. Once a rapport and trust is established, they will bring sexual experiences into the online conversation, ask the child to send sexual photographs and even try to meet them.

Grooming can also take place via computer gaming. Breck Bednar was a 14-year-old boy who loved technology and online gaming. He was groomed and manipulated by someone he played online games with and he went to meet them without his parents' knowledge. He was murdered by that person on 17 February 2014. His parents have set up *The Breck Foundation* in his memory, which seeks to raise awareness of playing safe while using the Internet.[120]

Thankfully these cases are rare, but as parents we need to be vigilant about safeguarding our children against online grooming.

---

119 Internet Matters, 'From Survive to Thrive: Supporting digital family life after lockdown'.
120 *The Breck Foundation*, charity registration no. 1168384, breckfoundation.org.

WHAT PARENTS CAN DO

✓ Use parental controls and filters
Monitor and limit what your children can access on their devices (see appendix for more information).

✓ Talk about it
As with all the potential dangers for children from digital technology, it's important that we keep a sense of perspective as parents: obviously not all new contacts on social media or gaming sites are paedophiles or murderers. But we mustn't bury our heads in the sand either. Encouragingly, one trend which emerged from the pandemic is that parents report more engagement with their children's online activities, and in particular, increased confidence in taking action to keep their children safe online.[121]

In the same way as dealing with the issues of porn and sexting, it is never too early to begin a conversation with our children. Talk to younger children about grooming in the same way as you would 'stranger danger'. They should not talk privately or give personal information to anyone they don't know, whether in real life or online. Make sure they know what 'personal information' is. Talk to them about the sites they use, what sorts of conversations they have and the information they share. Keeping the lines of communication open (not easy with monosyllabic teenagers) is key, so that we can make sure they are clearly aware of the dangers. In particular, we can caution them against disclosing any personal details or arranging a face-to-face meeting with someone they don't know. Our children need to know that people online aren't always who they make out they are.

Older children may well not want to be forthcoming with us about their social networks, and we'll want them to have their privacy without feeling that we are interfering. Take advantage of websites such as www.ceop.police.uk for advice about how to communicate with them (see appendix for more information).

---

121 Internet Matters, 'From Survive to Thrive: Supporting digital family life after lockdown'.

We also need to remind our children that they should never arrange to meet someone they only know online without an adult they trust.

Research demonstrates that children facing offline vulnerabilities are more at risk online, and their offline vulnerabilities inform which type of risks they will encounter online.[122] This will, in all likelihood, be the lived experience of many parents and carers of vulnerable children, who will be aware of the increased need to be vigilant and ensure the right safety nets are in place. One dad with a son, aged 13, reflected, 'with my child being special needs, the responsibility lies with me to ensure my child is "online" safe'.[123]

✓ Watch out for changes in your child's behaviour

Unusual changes in our children's behaviour can be warning signs that they might be victims of grooming. One website, www. internetmatters.org, suggests that these may include the following:

- Wanting to spend more and more time on the Internet.
- Being secretive about who they are talking to online and what sites they visit.
- Switching screens when you come near the computer.
- Possessing items – electronic devices or phones – you haven't given them.
- Using sexual language you wouldn't expect them to know.
- Becoming emotionally volatile.[124]

Of course, secretive, emotional and 'unusual' behaviour is fairly typical of teenagers, so we shouldn't assume the worst, but if we do find our children have been the victim of grooming (our children may not even realize that's what it is) then, like Kayleigh's mother, we should contact the police.

122 Adrienne Katz and Aiman El Asam, 'Refuge and Risk: Life Online for Vulnerable Young People', *Internet Matters*, 2021, internetmatters.org.
123 *Ibid.*
124 Internet Matters, 'How do I protect my child from being groomed?', *Internet Matters Resources*, 2021, internetmatters.org.

✓ Be there for them

Let your children know that they can come to you, or another adult they trust at any time, if they get into trouble online or are worried about any conversations they may be having with people.

If you think that your child is being groomed or in immediate danger, report it to the police at once. You can also call the NSPCC's free adult helpline or the National Crime Agency's CEOP Command (see appendix for further information).

'How about you go read some parenting books
and just let me play?'

CHAPTER 13

INTERNET ADDICTION

At the end of our Care for the Family seminars, one of the frequent concerns that parents want to discuss with us is possible Internet addiction. The increase in screen use during the pandemic served to heighten anxiety: one survey revealed that over half of parents felt their child became too reliant on technology during lockdown.[125] Their concerns are not unfounded. Shocking reports have appeared in the media of children as young as 4 being addicted to iPads and smartphones. There is now an NHS clinic specifically for children and young adults with computer game addiction,[126] and according to Barnardo's, children aged 5 and under are at risk of becoming addicted to the Internet. Very young children – one as young as 2 – were learning to access websites as a result of their parents giving them access to smartphones or tablet computers to distract or entertain them. Such early access to electronic devices could lead to both addiction and a loss of key social skills as families spend less time talking among themselves.[127]

And children have gone to extraordinarily extreme lengths to ensure their online access. A 16-year-old American girl and her friend were so desperate to get around the 10pm family Internet curfew that they went out to the local shop, bought milkshakes for her parents, and mixed them with ground-up sleeping tablets. An hour later, the parents were slumbering peacefully leaving the girls free to use the Internet as they pleased. When the parents woke in the morning with terrific hangover-like symptoms, their suspicions were aroused and they bought a cheap drug testing kit to test

125 Internet Matters, 'From Survive to Thrive: Supporting digital family life after lockdown'.
126 NHS, 'Children treated for computer gaming addiction under NHS Long Term Plan,' *NHS News*, October 2019, nhs.uk.
127 Denis Campbell, 'Children age five and under at risk of internet addiction,' *The Guardian*, 10 June 2019.

themselves. Before they knew it, the girls were answering questions at the local police station.[128]

An article in the *New York Post* by Dr Nicholas Kardaras caused widespread concern among many anxious parents when he argued that young children exposed to too much screen time were at risk of developing an addiction 'harder to kick than drugs'.[129] He reported that recent brain-imaging research confirmed that glowing screens affect the brain's prefrontal cortex in the same way as drugs like cocaine and heroin. This is the part of the brain that controls impulse and mental functions and helps us manage time, pay attention, plan, organize and remember details. He also referred to research from the US military with burn victims. While their wounds were being dressed, they normally required large doses of morphine, but when they were given a video game to play they felt no pain. While a wonderful advance in pain-management, it begs the question as to what effect this digital 'drug' is having on the brains of over-stimulated 7-year-olds who are glued to their glowing screens. Perhaps, then, it's no surprise that Steve Jobs was a notoriously low-tech parent, as are many of Silicon Valley's top technology designers and engineers today.[130]

Anticipation and reward

The slot machine is the most profitable part of any casino: the sheer power of anticipation and reward locks users into an addictive cycle of play. It is these very same features of anticipation and reward that tech designers have harnessed to make social media so compelling. What drives us to check our notifications and to pull the lever of a slot machine are surprisingly similar, so much so that psychologists have dubbed it 'the slot machine effect'.

Slot machines are designed to draw us into the 'zone'. They encourage constant play, give positive reinforcement and pay out

---

128 Amanda Holpuch, 'California teens accused of drugging parents to get around internet curfew', *The Guardian*, 3 January 2013.
129 Nicholas Kardaras, 'It's "digital heroin": How screens turn kids into psychotic junkies'.
130 Chris Weller, 'Silicon Valley parents are raising their kids tech-free – and it should be a red flag', *Business Insider*, February 2018, businessinsider.com.

small regular wins to keep us engaged. Social media uses exactly the same features, but instead of money, it is designed to cost our time and attention. We live in what is now known as 'an attention economy', the invasive 'ping' of a message, coupled with the notification on our screens – an eye-catching shade of red – are all designed to grab our attention. (Incidentally setting your phone to 'greyscale' gives a graphic demonstration of how alluring these red notifications are; the screen of a black and white phone is not half as compelling!)

The same surprise element of reward that keeps people at the roulette wheel also keeps people eyeballing their screens. Each 'like' gives the social reward of approval, which triggers a dopamine surge, makes us feel good and leaves us wanting more. The very nature of 'likes' is that they are variable and therefore more compelling. We don't know at what time of the day or night they will come, which explains why some teens are even setting alarms for the early hours of the morning just to check how many 'likes' they have. The infinite scroll feature allows users to endlessly swipe through content; the brain has no time to catch up and no incentive to end the task.

Reflecting on her engagement with TikTok during lockdown, 15-year-old Alice described it as 'a bit of an addiction' while William (16) said, 'You go on it for five minutes, and then you end up scrolling for two hours. It's just addicting: once you get scrolling you just keep on doing it. I don't know what it is about.'[131]

Technology Companies have developed increasingly sophisticated algorithms that analyse what we search for, even what we write in our emails, to tailor the content we see to what we're interested in. Have you ever noticed being bombarded by adverts for holidays or hotels after searching for flights online? (For more on targeted advertising, see Chapter 14.)

Snapchat streaks are another example of these attention-grabbing features. A Snapchat streak begins when two friends have 'snapped' a picture or video to each other within twenty-four hours over three days. To keep the streak going, they must continue

131 Ofcom, 'Children's Media Lives 2020/21'.

to send a picture or video every single day. While a streak of ten days is relatively easy to break, the higher the number of days, the higher the stakes. Fifteen-year-old Sophie wasn't unusual in giving her phone to her friend while she was away on school camp and employing her simply to maintain her streak.

Bradley was given his first smartphone just before he started secondary school. Before long he also had a laptop (needed for homework) and, after much pleading, an iPad. While at a friend's house he was introduced to a gaming forum and started playing video games with online friends who he never met face to face. He began to spend more time online, often playing until the small hours of the morning. His parents and friends noticed a change in his behaviour; he became aggressive and distant, dropped his old friends, and his mum said he stopped playing football, going to church and joining in after-school activities altogether. Bradley needed help.

Although the possibility of online activity taking over our children's lives is a real one, we need to keep a sense of perspective. Children generally don't get addicted to digital technology simply by being in contact with it, and the addictive behaviour may be due to underlying issues such as gambling, shopping or other mental wellbeing challenges, rather than online activity itself. Like any addiction to drugs and alcohol, the Internet offers children and adolescents a way to escape problems, difficult situations and painful feelings. Children who don't have close friendships and who have poor social and coping skills are at greater risk of developing Internet addiction. Because they feel alone, alienated, and have problems making new friends, they may turn to invisible strangers online for the attention and companionship missing in their real lives – they create a comforting online world for themselves as a means of escape.

An extract from an entertaining article by journalist Katie Roiphe, helps keep things in perspective:

The other day, I did something that is, apparently, not done: I brought my seven-year-old and his friend to a playground while they were hunting for Pokémon on an iPhone. A strong ripple of disapproval ran through assorted benched parents ...

I've been noticing that some of the parents of my son's friends refuse to let their kids play Pokémon Go or Minecraft, and are mystified by or politely disapproving of my wanton permissiveness. 'We don't do that,' they say, in slightly the same tone they would use if I were letting seven-year-olds play tag in a needle-strewn crack den. In my small addict's defense, he does marshal impressive research skills in these endeavours. He has read every book on Minecraft in existence; at night he falls asleep studying Pokémon dictionaries. He is probably, I tell him, one of the world's leading experts on Pokémon …

Meanwhile, as I write, the small addict's 13-year-old sister – I'll call her the big addict – is sprawled languorously across a couch. I ask her what she is doing but she is too languorous to do much more than whisper a barely audible response. She is, however, able to raise her arm slightly for Snapchat. While I am aware that taking a weird picture of herself, with butterflies superimposed in her hair, and sending it to a friend with an inane comment is not the highest form of human connection, I can't say it's worse than the endless hours I used to spend on the phone with my friends, lying upside down on my bed, twirling the curly phone cord.

As Danah Boyd, an internet scholar, has pointed out, hanging out is part of the work of teenage years; socialising is part of learning to be a functional adult. In It's Complicated, Boyd writes, 'Teens turn to, and are obsessed with, whichever environment allows them to connect to friends. Most teens aren't addicted to social media; if anything, they're addicted to each other.'[132]

As parents, we'll understandably want our children not to miss out on the things that we did when we were young – making dens in the garden or tents with sheets draped over the living-room furniture, riding bikes, playing board games and having sleepovers – but we also don't want to prevent them from socializing and connecting with their peers. So how do we know when 'normal' activity crosses the invisible line into addictive use? How much is too much?

132 Katie Roiphe, 'Screen wars: parents v children', *Financial Times*, 16 December 2016.

'I can't tell if he's seriously addicted or just a typical teen ...'

Addiction is a state where someone compulsively engages with a stimulus (which might be drugs, alcohol, shopping, or – as here – online activity) in a way that interferes with normal everyday life. Simon, now a father of three, admits to having a computer addiction while at university. He said:

> *'My online activity took over my life. The more I was online the more I needed to be online to get another 'fix'. I was so immersed in my gaming that I would forget to eat and to sleep. I withdrew from flatmates and my studies began to suffer.'*

If we take a step back, we can see how online activity has all the raw ingredients necessary to encourage addictive behaviour, particularly with risk-taking, consequence-oblivious, impressionable teens. Addictions thrive on regular reward, generating the need for more and more, and then more again. Gaming manufacturers use this to their advantage; each stage is designed so that the player wants to go on to the next one. Social media, as well as gaming, also encourages compulsive behaviour by feeding an insatiable appetite for 'likes' and 'shares' fuelled by FOMO (fear of missing out). This can lead to checking social media feeds 24/7.

But let's not throw the baby out with the bathwater. It's worth repeating (as discussed in Chapter 7) that limited gaming can be of benefit to our children. One study found that young people who played games for an hour a day actually appeared *better* adjusted than those who didn't play games at all.[133] They had fewer social or emotional problems, were happier about their friendships, were more helpful to others and were generally more satisfied with life. However, the minority who played for more than three hours a day seemed to be worse off. They were more likely to be hyperactive and emotionally volatile compared to those who played less or not at all. Those who played between one and three hours a day appeared no different to those who never played games. The principle we can

133 Andrew K. Przybylski, 'Electronic Gaming and Psychosocial Adjustment', *Pediatrics*, vol.134, no.3, September 2014.

take from this is that while we don't need to rigidly set the number of minutes our children spend gaming, as parents we ignore their excessive screen use at our peril.

Even more encouraging for those of us who are somewhat weary in monitoring our children's screen time was that research found that only about 2% of hyperactivity and antisocial behaviour could be related to gaming. Other factors such as schooling, housing and gender had a much bigger impact on children's well-being.

WHAT PARENTS CAN DO

✓ Find out what your child is doing online
If we believe our child may have an Internet addiction, it is worth finding out what it is that they are doing online. We may discover that their behaviour online is actually the result of an addiction to another activity (gambling or shopping, for example). If that is the case, we will need to seek the appropriate help for them.

✓ Put screen time guidelines in place (see Chapter 4)
On one of our recent parenting courses, we discovered that some teenagers were online for as long as thirty-one hours a week. Having limitations on screen time is a key strategy in combating Internet addiction. Particularly at the younger end of the teenage years, it's essential to have some clear guidelines in place. Consider keeping a diary with your child of their Internet use (most smartphones have apps that can help with this too). This will help you both learn if there are times when they use it more, or triggers that cause them to stay online a long time.

✓ Talk about it
Talk with your child about the amount of time they are spending on the Internet and try to find out if there are specific reasons for this. Sometimes it can offer an escape from reality, and there may be problems that they are trying to get away from. If your child is

facing problems that are causing this desire to escape, try to address those.

✓ Watch out for signs of excessive Internet use
1. Losing track of time while online and forgetting to eat or to sleep. The gaming, texting or social media becomes all-consuming.
2. Withdrawal – feelings of tension, anger, or depression when they do not have access to the computer.
3. Tolerance – becoming increasingly resistant or tolerant to the benefits they get from the Internet. Eventually they want to spend more hours online or feel they need better software or computers.
4. Negative repercussions – arguments, lies, social isolation, tiredness and low achievement.

✓ When Things Go Wrong
Despite our best efforts at safeguarding our children, we may find ourselves in a situation where the Internet does seem to have taken over our child's life. One mum described how she believed her 15 and 12-year-old sons are both completely addicted:

'Screen time dictates their entire lives; without it they are raging wrecks. As soon as they get out of bed, and absolutely whenever they can, and often when they shouldn't, they're gaming or on Instagram, Snapchat or Twitter. My 15-year-old is often up until 2am. I go to bed, tell him his phone must be off, but he waits until I'm sleeping and then switches it back on. Our whole lives revolve around it … It affects us all [as a family]. My husband gets angry and feels I undermine him when he tries to act. And I suppose I do, partly because switching things off causes such a lot of aggravation … he just walks away and leaves the kids to yell at me until I give in because I am too stressed to deal with it.'

Understandable reactions for parents seeing the signs of Internet addiction in their child are anger and fear. We might react by confiscating the offending digital device as a form of punishment or forcing our child to go 'cold turkey' to stop the problem. Neither of these responses are ideal, inviting our child to see us as the enemy, creating a 'them and us' atmosphere, and possibly resulting in them experiencing real withdrawal symptoms. It is much better to try and work *with* them by talking to them about the effect the amount of time they spend on screen has on both them and the family.

Tell them you love them, that you care about their happiness and that you are not blaming or condemning them but are concerned about what's happening – mention specific things you have noticed about their behaviour, such as fatigue, nervousness, giving up hobbies, etc. Next, decide what the boundaries will be for limited Internet use. If at all possible, do this together, especially with teenagers. This will be much easier said than done (but worth it in the end) as the very idea of limited screen time will be very difficult for them to manage.

Before we all rush to disable the Wi-Fi and gather up our offspring's games consoles, laptops and smartphones to put in the recycling, once again, let me give a caveat: if we have teenagers in the house, we may recognize some of these symptoms as an integral part of normal teenage behaviour – unrelated to potential addiction problems. But, as their parents, we know our child best. We are in the very best position to know whether their behaviour has changed, has disrupted family life sufficiently to have crossed the line, and is a cause for concern.

If our children are showing signs of addictive behaviour, it is important to get help. If you feel that your advice is falling on deaf ears, consider involving others – such as respected family friends, youth leaders, or sports coaches – who they may listen to. And don't be afraid to seek professional help – your GP is the most obvious place to start.

CHAPTER 14

CONSUMER CULTURE

In 1960, Professor Walter Mischel of Stanford University began the first of a series of famous studies that have come to be known as 'The Marshmallow Experiment'. Taking a group of children aged 4–6, a researcher sat them down individually in a room free of distractions and put a marshmallow (or another treat of their choice) on a table by a chair. The researcher explained that they were going to leave the room and return in about fifteen minutes. If the child waited and didn't eat the marshmallow until he came back in, they would earn a second marshmallow; if they ate it before he came back in, they would not be given a second one. A simple deal: one marshmallow now or two later. Mischel reported that some children ate their treat as soon as the researcher left the room, but others:

> … cover their eyes with their hands or turn around so that they can't see the tray, others start kicking the desk, or tug on their pigtails, or stroke the marshmallow as if it were a tiny stuffed animal.[134]

In follow-up studies, the researchers found unexpected correlations between the results of the marshmallow test and the success of the children many years later, in all kinds of ways. Those who had been able to wait in order to receive the reward of the second treat tended to have better life outcomes as measured by educational attainment, SAT scores, body mass index and other life measures.

This simple experiment revealed what is now believed to be one of the most important factors that contribute to success in life: the power of delayed gratification.

---

134 Walter Mischel, et al., 'Cognitive and attentional mechanisms in delay of gratification', *Journal of Personality and Social Psychology*, vol.21, no.2, 1972, pp204–218.

'What do you mean you ate them all?! You knew
we were going to do the marshmallow test on the
kids today!'

As parents, we will want to teach our children the advantages of delayed gratification – short-term pain for long-term gain! However, in this endeavour we are not taking part on a level playing field. We are competing against a culture which continually bombards them with the opposite message. One click on Amazon Prime from their phones 'takes the waiting out of wanting' and offers instant satisfaction.

Last night, I spent some time on my laptop googling vintage metal light fittings. Hoping for a hallway that rivals some of those seen on Pinterest, I set out to compare and contrast what was on offer in this admittedly niche market. This morning I am being pestered and pursued by every light fitting manufacturer known to man.

Perhaps even more intriguing, returning from holiday a while ago I packed a bottle of red wine in our suitcase, cushioned (as I thought) between our swimming towels. Sadly, some energetic baggage handling at the airport resulted in the bottle exploding, with an ensuing overpowering bouquet of Rioja and a suitcase of pink clothes. Once home, I tweeted about our experience and seconds later a message came into my inbox letting me know about the Jet Bag which promised to be 'the diaper for the wine in your luggage'.

It's what is known as personal targeted advertising, and it is directed just as much at brand-conscious young consumers as their adult counterparts. Social media is punctuated with sponsored advertising giving incentives to buy those must-have trainers, fake eyelashes, favourite music track, Xbox game or props for avatars. Teens are also increasingly using their own networks for sharing information about the latest fashion essential or once-in-a-lifetime bargain. Those of us with teenage daughters will no doubt be familiar with the phenomenon of hundreds of photos taken from assorted angles in changing rooms as different clothes are being tried on. These pictures are then sent around their friends for admiration and comment. With shops closed for long periods of time during lockdown, parents reported a 42% increase in spending online, which included online shopping as well as game credits and app purchases. Parents of vulnerable children reported a 64% increase.[135]

135 Internet Matters, 'From Survive to Thrive: Supporting digital family life after lockdown'.

Of course, there is nothing new about children wanting things – new toys, gadgets, cosmetics snacks or clothes – but today's parents have a harder job to combat pester power than in previous generations because of the 24/7 presence of advertising and media through digital technology. The 'Letting Children Be Children' review, which described the commericalization and sexualization of children, reported that:

> Nearly nine out of ten parents surveyed for this Review agreed with the statement that 'these days children are under pressure to grow up too quickly' … This pressure on children to grow up takes two different but related forms: the pressure to take part in a sexualised life before they are ready to do so; and the commercial pressure to consume the vast range of goods and services that are available to children and young people of all ages.[136]

Kids' advertising spending is increasing, with 2021 estimates at 4.6 billion U.S. dollars, out of which 1.7 billion is from digital advertising formats.[137] However, the recognized impact of online media on young people is possibly less about advertising and the pressure to buy, buy, buy and more about 'brand and lifestyle'. Many older children are increasingly savvy and recognize the power of commercial sales and marketing, but the subtle pressure of a makeup demonstration on YouTube or an Instagram fashionista modelling the latest trends may be more difficult to recognize and resist.

Online games can offer instant upgrades while your children are playing them – so if the account is set up in your name and the bill is paid by you, that summer holiday to Spain might be in jeopardy. My brother found to his cost that it just takes a moment to run up a crazy bill:

136 Reg Bailey, 'Letting Children Be Children. Report of an Independent Review of the Commercialisation and Sexualisation of Childhood'.
137 A. Guttman, 'Spending on advertising to children worldwide from 2012–2021', *Statista*, April 2020, statista.com.

'Good afternoon, madam. You were just googling "How to remove carpet stains". Can I show you the SuckCleaner 2000? It's a complete cleaning system for all your cleaning needs ...'

'Our 13-year-old used his first phone for messaging his friends and playing games. There were a couple of apps on it that not only allowed him to play games but invited him to click 'yes' to various premium lines. At the end of the month, I was horrified to receive a bill for £340. A call to Watchdog made the phone company spring into action and refund the money, but the result could have been so different. A timely lesson learnt by us all.'

As mentioned in Chapter 7, in-app purchases can also catch us unawares. Games that are 'free-to-play' may be free to download and play on a basic level, but the catch is that you have to spend money to improve the game experience – to move up a level, for example. Often it is the only way to compete if you are playing against another person who has spent money on the game. Some in-app purchases can even be renewable, like monthly subscriptions that repeat until you cancel them.

Another issue is the ease with which young people online can pull the wool over the eyes of suppliers about their age. While it may be difficult for most fresh-faced 15-year-olds to buy that bottle of vodka at the local off-licence – even with fake ID – underage purchases are made with apparent ease online. I remember setting up a family investigation to rival Scotland Yard's best efforts after an over-18 game mysteriously arrived in the post; the only people in the house older than 18 were my husband and myself, and we certainly hadn't placed the order.

But while it can be stressful and expensive for their parents, how harmful is a child's increased exposure to consumer pressures? A British study found that consumerism is not a benign influence on our children and that it can result in them being depressed and anxious.[138] Further evidence also suggests that children who place a high value on what they own have a greater tendency for depression as well as loneliness, insecurity, general discontentment and social

138 'The good childhood – a national inquiry: evidence summary four – lifestyle', *The Children's Society*, 2008, childrenssociety.org.uk.

problems.[139] They are more likely to believe that possessions bring happiness, that success is defined by what they own, and that the primary goal in life is to acquire material goods and the admiration of others.

WHAT PARENTS CAN DO

✓ Remember that young children are particularly vulnerable to advertising

Research suggests that until the ages of about 7 or 8, children do not understand the true purpose of advertisements – seeing it as another form of entertainment or information-sharing.[140] When 8–11-year-olds were presented with an image of a Google search for children's trainers, less than half understood that the results appearing with the prefix 'Ad' were only there because they had paid to be listed.[141] One researcher pointed out that younger children 'aren't even able to understand that ads, which are now cropping up in video games and movies, online and even in cell phones, are intended to sell them things'.[142] Unsurprisingly, perhaps, the researchers discovered that the more time California third graders spent watching TV or playing video games, the more often they asked an adult to buy them the items they saw on the screen.

✓ Limit their exposure

Use parental controls to actively monitor your children's online screen time (see Chapter 4).

---

139 Donna Bee-Gates, 'Consumer Culture: Confronting materialism while raising children', *Parentguide News*, parentguidenews.com.

140 Karen J. Pine, Penny Wilson and Avril Nash, 'The Relationship Between Television Advertising, Children's Viewing and Their Requests to Father Christmas', *Journal of Developmental & Behavioral Pediatrics*, vol.28, no.6, 2007, pp456–461.

141 Ofcom, 'Children and parents: media use and attitudes report 2020'.

142 Christa Conger, 'Watch not, want not? Kids' TV time tied to consumerism', *Stanford Medicine News Center*, 3 April 2006, stanford.edu.

✓ Talk about spending

It's never too early to talk to our children about money and the relentless pressure to buy, and learning to shop both offline and online teaches important lessons for life. We can give pocket money for sweets or toys when they are little, teaching them to budget and to save (learning that all-important quality of delayed gratification), and then allowing them more responsibility with money as they get older. We can have family discussions about the pitfalls of online shopping – hidden delivery costs, fake websites, the possibility of stolen bank account details – and we can let them know that if a bargain seems like it's too good to be true, it probably is. Remember that the more informed a child is about money, the less likely they are to spend it unthinkingly or as a means of comfort when under emotional pressure.

✓ Give them your time

A recent ONS report tells us that:

> The principal themes identified in relation to what children need for a happy life were: positive relationships, safe spaces and things to do, health and wellbeing, skills and schools, basic needs and a happy future. Love and affection featured strongly among the essentials for children's happiness - specifically, supportive family relationships and quality family time. It was agreed that although money provides comfort, stability and a better head start in life, which are all important for children to have a happy life … It might give you things that you want, but not … true happiness.[143]

✓ Help your children become media-savvy

Over the age of around 7 or 8, children are able to understand about advertising tactics, so start talking to them about this early on. Explain that adverts are created by companies to make people believe their products are going to make us feel better, have more

---

143 Amber Jordan and Eleanor Rees, 'Children's views on well-being and what makes a happy life, UK: 2020', *Office for National Statistics*, October 2020, ons.gov.uk.

fun, be prettier, be stronger, or make life better in some other way. They also make people think they need or want something that they never knew about and now feel they must have – right now!

Some of our friends used to play what they called 'the advert game' with their children. When an advertisement appears on screen, they have a competition to be the first to spot the 'lie' in the promotion.

You can help your children become more media-savvy by looking together at an online advertisement that they know well and asking them what it is doing to make the product seem like something they need. Does the advert make it look bigger than in real life (often the case with toy adverts)? Do the people look happy (suggesting that you would be happy if you had the product)? Does the advert feature famous actors, singers or sports personalities to make you think the product is good? Does it promote the product by giving you something for free with it, or scare you by saying that you need to hurry to buy it before the 'sale ends'?

With older children, help them think about how the advert was targeted at them. Is it based on the content of other sites they have visited (contextually targeted)? Or is it targeted at them because of online information about them – searches they have made, online purchases, browsing history (behaviourally targeted)? Ask them to search a term on their own device, and then to search the same term on your device and see if the results are different. Children can be really surprised when they realize how their personal information and actions determine what adverts they see.

Also with older children, talk about the way adverts sell ideas as well as products – for example, how they link products with the 'perfect' life portrayed by the people in the adverts, or with a happy family life, or a romantic relationship … [ask them to fill in the blanks].

'They play so well together ...'

CHAPTER 15

ALL KINDS OF FAMILIES –
ALL KINDS OF ISSUES

Families come in all shapes and sizes, and digital technology will bring different benefits and concerns in different parenting situations. In this chapter, we're going to look at some common family situations.

Carol and Ben are the parents of 13-year-old Tom.

Scene 1. In the car: From the moment she picks Tom up from school, Carol knows that it's going to be a long evening. Ignoring the grumpy face and brooding silence in the back, she asks brightly how his day has been. Experience has given her low expectations as to his response. He doesn't disappoint.

Scene 2. At home: The evening goes as anticipated: rows over hanging up his coat, homework, turning off the TV and sitting down at the table for tea. An innocent remark from his sister results in Tom kicking her on the shins and sending her flying backwards. Carol finally snaps. She dispatches Tom to his bedroom and tells him his games console is confiscated until the next day, and, in any event, until he apologizes to his sister.

Scene 3. Enter Ben: Ben has had a good day at work and is looking forwarding to catching up with the children before they go to bed. Carol tells him what has happened, and he goes upstairs to chat to Tom.

Scene 4. Ten minutes later: Carol hears shouts of delight from the living room and pokes her head around the door only to see father and son engaged in a game of FIFA on the confiscated games console.

Scene 5. Eleven minutes later: Probably best left to the imagination!

If we are parenting together, it is vital that as far as possible we remain united on matters of discipline and boundaries. There have been many occasions when, in the heat of the moment, either Richard or I have meted out an all too draconian punishment – no Xbox until the end of the year (but it's only 1 January), no birthday party (but half the class have already been invited), no trip to the cinema (but it's with Granny and we have already bought the tickets). At such times, it takes all the willpower in the universe not to undermine the other parent by immediately stepping in and siding with the child. If we (or our partner) have acted hastily and imposed unilateral sanctions worthy of foreign office diplomacy, we need to try to step back, apologize where necessary and accept that there is scope for undoing them. We all make mistakes and act in the heat of the moment, and as long as it's not a daily occurrence, these moments give a great opportunity to model apology and forgiveness in the family.

Being united on discipline and boundaries is just as important when it comes to digital use. If there is a chink of light between you, most savvy 10-year-olds will be right in there and able to use it to their advantage. Giving a clear, consistent and united message as a couple brings security to family life.

For single parents, the task of monitoring our children's digital use can be particularly challenging. It's hard enough with two pairs of eyes and two pairs of hands, so with half that resource the task can be immense. Most of us, but especially those parenting on their own, will at some point have needed to sit our toddler in front of a screen simply in order to have a shower or take a work call. A single dad commented:

> 'Single parents often let their children stay online for longer so they can have some down time or just get things done. They may be exhausted and if their children ask for fifteen minutes and then fifteen minutes more, they may say yes just to have peace and quiet. I've learnt not to go on a guilt trip, but once in a while try finding something non-digital to keep them quiet while you just catch up on jobs.'

Looking back to when her son was younger, another single parent talked about the benefits that digital technology has given them both:

'I remember when we bought my son his first mobile. He was still in junior school, and I thought at the time that he was too young to own a phone. However, all his friends had one, and as a parent, you want your children to be able to keep up to date with technology as the world progresses. Maybe I was being too old-fashioned, I thought. Fast forward a year from this date, and I am now a single parent. For me in this situation, my son owning a mobile phone is something that I rely on to communicate with him. I can contact him when he is at his dad's, when I'm at work – anytime, and my son can contact me.

As a single parent, you can't be everywhere all the time, and technology has helped me to be able to stay in contact in a way that I wouldn't have been able to in the past, before mobile phones. Using technology has helped me to have more peace of mind as I can communicate with my children, know they are okay, and know they can contact me at any time.'

Kat told me that she wasn't very tech-savvy when she became a single parent. She could use a computer, but as far as parental controls and security settings were concerned, she really didn't have a clue. Desperately wanting to protect her family online but not knowing how to go about doing it, she attended an evening her daughter's school was running for parents on Internet safety.

'The teachers spoke to us about how to place parental controls on our computers and told us about software that we could get to keep an eye on what the children were accessing online and who they were speaking to. I contacted a friend who was a computer technician and asked him to install it onto my children's laptop. I would strongly encourage any parent to go to any event like the one I went to, especially single parents as we don't have someone at home who can help us with these things.'

Many of the challenges single parents face are not because they are parenting alone: they are issues common to *every* parent. But life can be tough as a single mum or dad. Having less time and ability to supervise children's online activity, as well as setting and defending the boundaries alone isn't easy. If you are parenting alone, don't be afraid to ask for and accept help.

Many single parents or blended families may be trying to keep an eye on digital use across two households. Having consistent guidelines and safeguards is particularly helpful – and lots of parents in this situation are able to put this in place effectively. Sometimes, however, these arrangements don't run smoothly. Jon's children spend half the week with him and the other half with their mum and her partner. Jon reflects:

'We divorced when the kids were quite young, so they are used to dividing their week between both homes, but it has got more difficult as they have got older. Their mum's partner has older children from a previous relationship, and I find they are playing 15+ games there, which our kids are not old enough to do. It's hard as they are spending half the week in a place with different values and where you have no control.'

Lisa had a similar experience:

'My ex was the typical permissive parent. He gave the children no boundaries at all, and he encouraged them to watch movies or play games that they weren't allowed to watch in my home because they were not appropriate for their age. I tried to discuss creating some digital ground rules that we could agree so that the children had boundaries across both homes and wouldn't get confused. I would always stress that this was for our children's well-being and the focus was on them, not us. Unfortunately, the majority of the time, my ex was never too interested in laying down boundaries. He wanted to be the children's 'friend' and parented in this manner.

'Hi, Dad. Yes, I'm still at nursery, but there's a problem!
Sarah won't share the toys again. Can you come and
sort it out?'

In view of this, I had to decide what to do in my home. Should I allow my children to play video games and watch movies that were inappropriate for their age? Should I let them go online as much as they liked? I eventually decided that I would continue to keep the boundaries that I felt were right for the wellbeing, safety and protection of my children. I often wondered if I was doing the right thing and whether I was being too strict. My friends were a great support to me, encouraged me to hold the line, and said that even if my ex had a different approach these boundaries would help my children in the long run. I didn't always get it right, but overall, while I could not control what happened at their dad's house, I could control what happened in mine.'

If you are co-parenting, if at all possible, try to agree some guidelines for digital use that can be consistently applied in both homes. This will be easier to do in some situations than in others, especially if you initially have differing views, but if you can come to an agreement, it will be a win-win for the children and for you both. Some co-parenting situations are very challenging, so that kind of negotiation may not always be possible. It certainly isn't for the faint-hearted and may involve some give and take on both sides.

Foster parents can face a particular challenge when it comes to setting boundaries on technology use. Jon Trew, a foster parent himself and trainer in child protection and safety online, describes the problem in *Vodafone magazine*:

Newly fostered children often arrive with mobile devices they've brought from their previous home. They may have been allowed to view unsuitable material or to stay up late online ... It can be a challenge to change such habits, but it's not impossible. It's best to establish ground rules regarding online time immediately, just as you would with any other house rules. It's also important to be realistic: telling a child that they can use the computer only where you can see them isn't going to work in the mobile age![144]

144 Vodafone, 'Digital Parenting', *Vodafone magazine*, 2021, vodafone.com.

It is estimated that there are currently five million grandparents in the UK who provide childcare for their grandchildren,[145] and many more are in close regular contact with them. A grandparent can be the voice of reassurance and reason, speaking wisdom into children's lives over the years. Whether it's the 6-year-old who wants a sexy bra and high heels to look like her favourite singer on the latest music video, the 10-year-old who has stumbled across porn, or the image-conscious but slightly overweight 14-year-old who has been blocked by her best friend on TikTok, grandparents can give their grandchildren the most precious of gifts: the reassurance that they are loved simply for who they are.

Whether grandparents engage with their grandchildren face to face or across the miles, use of digital devices will almost certainly play a part. If grandparents are doing hands-on childcare, however informal the arrangement, the generation gap can result in a difference of opinion about digital use, so communication about the boundaries is key. Each family is different, but if the friction isn't easily resolved, giving grandparents the freedom (within limits) to agree digital guidelines when they are in charge, or at the very least when the children are in their home, might be a good place to start.

Modern technology makes grandparenting at a distance easier than ever, and those who are separated geographically from their grandchildren sometimes have as much interaction with them as those who live nearby. My mother is a great texter. She has a phone with a big enough screen to see easily, and she tells me she prefers texting to phoning as she doesn't worry that she is interrupting; but most of all it gives her a great means of connection with the wider family, especially her grandchildren and even her great grandchildren.

During lockdown many grandparents became proficient at using Zoom overnight. Liz, grandmother of five said:

'We set up a regular Zoom with our grandchildren on Friday afternoons during lockdown. The little ones spent most of the

---

145 'Later Life in the UK 2019', *Age UK*, May 2019, ageuk.org.uk.

*time bouncing on the sofa, but with the older ones we managed
to play snakes and ladders and read stories – all via a screen.
It was such a great way to stay in touch that we're carrying on
even though restrictions have lifted.'*

Technology offers other creative ways of communication. A
newspaper article from *The Times* had the title, 'Dear Granny,
thanks for my present. Love from me and my new app'.[146] Digital
card manufacturers have created software that can not only print
a personal picture on a card, but replicate the child's handwriting
and have it delivered on their behalf. Gone are the days of enforced
writing of thank-you letters to grandparents on Boxing Day (or
in our case, 15 January). A friend who is a wonderful granny
had a birthday card created by her 8-year-old granddaughter on
an iPad. While it admittedly couldn't join the array of cards on
the mantelpiece, she loved the time and effort that had gone into
creating it.

One granny we know has written a lovely story with her
grandson. She would write a paragraph and email it to him, and
then he would write the next bit and so on. It was not only a fun
activity for him, but built what is now a very special relationship
between them.

146 Fariha Karim, 'Dear Granny, thanks for my present. Love from me and my new app',
The Times, 6 January 2017.

CHAPTER 16

'SHARENTING' AND ROLE MODELS

A toddler licks out the icing bowl and, with chocolate smeared from ear to ear, grins at his mother. It is a delightful scene. Seconds later, an image (filtered 'vivid warm' to look as cute as possible) is beamed beyond the four walls of 16 Maple Avenue and circulated to the mum's 800+ Facebook followers and friends.

Welcome to the world of 'sharenting': parents sharing – and arguably oversharing – pictures, videos and the latest news about their offspring.

Talia had a digital footprint before she was born; even her twelve-week scan had winged its way across the Internet. By the time she was 5 years old, family, friends and complete strangers had viewed her first smile, first steps, first tooth, first birthday and first real tantrum. Over 500 images had been posted – including the time she missed the potty in the early days of potty training; a record of her life, without her consent.

Eighty-one per cent of children have an online presence before the age of 2,[147] and the average parent posts almost 1,500 images of their child before their fifth birthday.[148] Many 13-year-olds, on signing up to a social media account, are surprised to discover that they already have a digital footprint that they knew nothing about and had little to do with creating.

While some children are happy with their parents posting pictures, others are less so. Actress Gwyneth Paltrow made the headlines when she posted a picture of her and her 14-year-old daughter, Apple Martin, skiing. The post received over 150,000 'likes', but Apple wasn't happy. She wrote on her Instagram account:

147 Stacy Steinberg, 'Sharenting: Children's Privacy in the Age of Social Media', *University of Florida*, 2017, scholarship.law.ufl.edu.
148 Megan Rose, 'The average parent shares almost 1,500 images of their child online before their 5th birthday', *Parentzone*, 2021, parentzone.org.uk.

'Mom, we have discussed this. You may not post anything without my consent.' Paltrow replied, 'You can't even see your face!'[149]

Fourteen-year-old Sonia Bokari writes:

> When I saw the pictures that [my mother] had been posting on Facebook for years, I felt utterly embarrassed, and deeply betrayed. There, for anyone to see on her public Facebook account, were all of the embarrassing moments from my childhood: The letter I wrote to the tooth fairy when I was 5 years old, pictures of me crying when I was a toddler, and even vacation pictures of me when I was 12 and 13 that I had no knowledge of.[150]

Not all young people feel as strongly. Charlotte Christy, a 23-year-old student said:

> I think I share photos of my mum just as much as she shares photos of me – I think it's a natural thing to share and I don't see why she should ask for my permission – she's my mum.[151]

Celebrities' Instagram accounts reveal different attitudes to posting pictures of their children online. Holly Willoughby, George Clooney and Rio Ferdinand are just a few who want to protect their children. If they do post pictures, they ensure that they are taken from behind or that their faces are pixelated.[152] Other celebs have been less discreet, posting often, and even being accused of editing the shape of their children's noses or slimming down the puppy fat. The practice of editing photos has been rightly criticized, but maybe we shouldn't be so quick to point the finger. While we might not manipulate photos to make our children's noses smaller or eyes

149 Helier Cheung, 'Can you stop your parents sharing photos of you online?', *BBC News*, 28 March 2019, bbc.co.uk.
150 Sonia Bokhari, 'I'm 14 and I quit social media after discovering what was posted about me', *Fast Company Magazine*, March 2019, fastcompany.com.
151 Helier Cheung, 'Can you stop your parents sharing photos of you online?'.
152 'Sharenting: Holly Willoughby and Robbie Williams against the idea', *BBC Newsround*, 12 February 2019, bbc.co.uk.

bigger, many of us apply a 'filter' in terms of the message we seek to convey through our posts.

There is great pressure to post the highlights and show reels of blissfully happy family life. One mum recently commented that a friend had posted her child's school report on Facebook. I assume it contained lots of A*s and comments of 'excellent work', but it begs the question of whether she would have been so quick to post a report containing E's, F's or 'could do better'.

Family life is full of special moments which it is good to enjoy and to share. Technology enables us to keep a digital record of precious memories. Of course we will be proud of our children, and will want to celebrate them and their successes, but before our thumb hits the 'share' button, it might be worth pausing to consider our motives.

We know that the cute picture of our 6-year-old playing the ukulele could go viral, but who are we really doing it for? Parenting is not a competition. If we only share edited pictures that present our family in the best possible light, or obsess over our total number of 'likes', we will communicate to our children that their self-worth is tied to 'likes', and that their value lies in approval from others, rather than in who they were made to be.

As well as digital footprints, another aspect of 'sharenting' that has raised concerns is parents inadvertently sharing personal information that makes their children vulnerable. Posting a picture of a child outside their home, at the nursery gate or wearing their school blazer could lead to them being identified, and opens the door to the possibility of 'digital kidnapping', where strangers use publicly available photographs of children for fraudulent or sexual purposes.

WHAT PARENTS CAN DO

✓ Ask them

If they are old enough, have a conversation with your child about what (if any) photographs they are happy for you to share on a public forum. Agree some guidelines as part of your family media agreement (see Chapter 4).

✓ Respect your child's feelings

In particular, check that your post won't cause embarrassment or upset. One mum entered a competition for 'the untidiest bedroom' and was mortified to find the photograph of her daughter's bedroom on the front page of the local paper.

Many parents are increasingly asking grandparents, family and friends to refrain from posting pictures of their children on social media. If you are sharing a photo with another child in it, check that their parents are happy.

✓ Check privacy settings and turn off 'Geotagging'

Review the settings on your social media account so you know who can see your photos. You might want to consider setting up a private group. Remove location metadata to ensure that you are not inadvertently revealing personal information – including the GPS coordinates or the date and of the photograph – that could lead to your child being easily identified.

✓ Celebrate your child

But remember, parenting isn't a competition. Think before you share!

ROLE MODELS AND DISTRACTED PARENTS

I had a fascinating conversation recently with a friend. She has three lively children and they had just been out for a pizza. While paying the bill, she apologized to the waitress for the commotion and mess at their table. She couldn't have been more surprised by the response: 'Please don't apologize – we love it. In fact, we play a game where we try to spot the two types of families that eat with us. There are the silent tables – they make no noise and no mess, no-one is speaking and they are all on screens – and then there are families like yours!' My friend wasn't entirely sure whether this was a compliment, but nevertheless went home reassured.

These days, whenever I go out for a meal, I make it a habit to look around. Pretty soon my eyes will fall on a table; the kids will be on iPads – which isn't unusual – but increasingly I notice that the parents are also engrossed in screens.

The phrase 'Smartphone orphans' has been used to describe a generation of children whose parents are distracted by technology. We know that there are huge advantages to having that smartphone in our pocket, but with all these advantages come some insidious dangers. While I imagine you have picked up this book hoping for some wisdom on how to manage your children's screen time, the uncomfortable truth is that one of the lessons may be closer to home. We are role models in how we use technology.

If the first thing we do when we come home from work is pick up our phone; if we are scrolling through messages while listening to them read; if we are engrossed in our phone while watching them swim, they will notice. The mantra 'do what I say and not what I do' just doesn't hold water; they will take their cue from us.

The pandemic created further complications. Working from home has meant that though we might be in the same room as our children, we are not emotionally available to them. During lockdown, when parents were valiantly juggling home-schooling and homeworking, this was to some extent unavoidable. There may have been emails that needed urgent attention and Zoom conference calls that wouldn't wait. But as restrictions lift and we return to some kind of normality we may find checking in on our work accounts at all times of the day and night has become a habit. For many, homeworking has blurred the lines between family time and work time, which can be confusing for children.

Psychologists now use the phrase 'technoference' to describe the phenomenon of phones getting in the way of engaging with our children. We can be physically present, but emotionally absent. I remember being deeply moved on hearing a little girl explain how she felt when her parents were on the phone. A wistful look came into her eyes as she said, 'I sometimes want to play a board game, but Mummy is too busy on her phone. It makes me feel sad. I feel like she doesn't care.'

While filming Care for the Family's DVD course, *Parentalk in the Primary Years*, we interviewed Jon, a dad with two boys aged

8 and 10. He had a demanding job and took full advantage of his smartphone's 24/7 access to his emails to help him keep his inbox under control. One of his boys, however, saw Jon's phone in a different light. One Saturday morning as Jon was replying to some emails, he heard his son asking him a question, but wasn't really listening and so didn't reply. His son persisted, 'Daddy, can we go to the park? ... Daddy ... ' Irritated, Jon looked up and said, 'Can't you see I'm busy?' In sheer frustration, his son replied, 'You're a much nicer daddy without your iPhone.' Ouch! For that young father, it was a wake-up call.

Journalist Katie Roiphe made a similar point when she wrote about her 7-year-old's observations:

> [He] often points out that in the exact moment I am telling him to get off his iPad, I am glancing at my email. He is rightfully outraged that my stupid addiction is somehow perfectly acceptable and even laudable adult behaviour, while his is rotting his brain. His addiction is somehow stunting him, dashing his attention span and perverting his ability to live in the moment but mine is just, you know, keeping up with the office and following political news in a responsible way.[153]

And it's not just younger children who can feel ignored. A third of 2,000 secondary school pupils surveyed had asked their parents to stop checking their devices.[154] Twenty-two per cent said that the use of mobiles stopped their families enjoying each other's company. Reflecting on this, Samantha, mum of five, said:

> *I realize now that when I am on my phone, all my children see is the back of the phone. They have no idea whether I am texting a friend, looking up a recipe for tea, trying to arrange a playdate for them or scrolling through Instagram. It all looks the same to them: the back of a screen.*

153 Katie Roiphe, 'Screen wars: parents v children'.
154 Judith Burns, 'Parents' mobile use harms family life, say secondary pupils', *BBC News*, 23 April 2017, bbc.co.uk.

In a recent study,[155] psychologists asked parents how often they thought their use of devices interrupted interactions with their child. Most agreed they were frequently distracted; only 11% claimed that they were unaffected. In the same experiment, the parents were asked to rate their children's behaviour. Did they sulk, display easily hurt feelings or whinge? Were they hyperactive or easily frustrated? Did they have frequent temper tantrums? The findings were interesting: the more often parents reported themselves as being distracted from their children by their devices, the more behavioural issues they noticed their children having.

This is a stark reminder that we need to consider our own phone use before addressing our children's. Part of the problem is that technology is so easily accessible, prevalent and unpredictable. We are at the mercy of a beep from a text or notification, and we get a buzz out of it.

It is said of parenting that 'the days are long, but the years are short'. The time goes so very quickly. If we look back in twenty years' time at the things that distracted us from giving our children the gift of time – that Amazon delivery notification, picture of the neighbour's cat or a news update – they may not seem so urgent after all. We might find ourselves asking, 'Why did I allow these things to rob me of even a minute of precious family time?'

Mobiles are not good mannered: they interrupt, shout, ping, screech and generally demand our attention now! It is no bad thing to give that ill-behaved device some 'time-out' and turn it off for a while. Life is busy, and we can't give our children 100% of our attention all the time. But when we can, let's really be with them, and put the phone away.

155 Brandon T. McDaniel and Jenny S. Radesky, 'Technoference: Parent Distraction with Technology and Associations With Child Behavior Problems', *Child Development*, vol.89, no.1, May 2017, researchgate.net.

CHAPTER 17

TEACHING THEM TO LEARN TO DISCERN

A family walk recently took us along a beautiful Pembrokeshire coastal path. It was a January day and the sky was bright blue with not a cloud in sight. We paused on the clifftop to enjoy the view. Stretching to the horizon in one direction was a patchwork of green fields, and in the other we could see the reassuring rhythm of the waves as they glistened in the winter sun. We breathed in the sea air … it was good to be alive.

After a few moments, we clambered down onto the beach and walked across the sand, making our way around the edge of a cliff. And then we saw it: a red flag fluttering in the breeze high up on the dunes. Our path had inadvertently taken us onto the MOD firing range. In a moment, the afternoon no longer felt so relaxed and carefree. We needed to pay attention and choose our route home rather more carefully.

I later reflected that this path, which offers its walkers such breathtaking scenery and new horizons, at the very same time has the potential to kill, harm and destroy unless it is followed very carefully. As parents, how do we teach our children to walk the path of digital engagement wisely, making the most of the incredible opportunities it offers while equipping them to steer clear of the dangers?

As we've discussed, there are age-appropriate external safeguards that we can put in place to protect our children which are absolutely vital, particularly when they are young: passwords, filters, parental controls, family media agreements. But those external controls simply aren't enough.

It was the first term at secondary school and one of our boys asked if he could go to a friend's birthday sleepover. We didn't know the parents well, but all his friends were going and we said yes. It was some time later that we found out that much of the time there had been spent looking at pornographic images on the dad's computer.

We can put every protection in the universe in place, our home can be a digitally impenetrable Fort Knox with every safeguard known to man installed, but it doesn't protect our children when they are away from home. In the playground, at a neighbour's house, in the changing rooms after a match, with a friend whose parents have different values to our own or who don't implement external safeguards themselves, there's the potential for them to download anything on the planet.

It is easy to feel overwhelmed by the dangers – real and imagined – that they may face living in a digital culture. But, as their parents we really are the biggest influence in our children's lives; bigger than any social media platform, YouTube video, or any game of the moment. There's so much to play for! And it's not 'one size fits all' – we can help them each find their own way to relate to technology.

It's been said that values are more often caught than taught. Sometimes we think our children aren't listening to us; in fact, the problem is quite the opposite. And we are role models to our children not just in how we use digital media but in every aspect of our lives. They notice the value that we place on relationships, on money, on the environment, on our health, on our possessions, on issues of faith, on how we treat others, particularly those who have less than we do. They don't miss a thing.

While there are no guarantees, little by little through the conversations, the time spent together and the everyday ups and the downs of family life, intentionally and unintentionally over the years we will be sowing values into our children's lives that will become the reference point for their own decision-making in the years to come.

Our role as parents is a positive one. We don't just have to leave our children to their own devices either in the digital world or the wider world. Instead of being naysayers, we can teach our children to manage their freedom well, training them from the inside out to make wise choices in a world where all choices are possible. We do this by placing values in their hearts that will be the compass for their lives. When we live out our values in the context of our family life, we'll be empowering our children with the confidence and wisdom not to just go with the flow, but empowering them to make good choices. To learn to discern.

The writer in the ancient book of Proverbs said this about wisdom:

> *Do not forsake wisdom, and she will protect you; love her, and she will watch over you.*[156]

The beginning of wisdom is this: get wisdom. That, I imagine, is what we want for all of our children.

---

156 The Holy Bible, New International Version, Proverbs 4:6.

'Time to turn that thing off now, Dad.
I think you're getting addicted to it ...'

EPILOGUE

The rain is hammering against Alice's bedroom window as she throws her schoolbag onto her bed. She can hear her little brothers squabbling downstairs. It's 7.15pm and already dark, so she draws the curtains. She has a school science project to complete and turns on her laptop. Before getting going, she notices that Karl is online. He is 15. Karl speaks first:

> Hi Alice. I've seen you on the bus. You're
> in the year below me, aren't you?
> **Yes.**
> You're very pretty.
> **Thank you.**
> Alice, undo the top three buttons on your
> shirt. [Long pause]

Alice's hand reaches for her top button. As she does, her mind goes back to a hundred conversations with her mum and her dad – over dinner, in the car, late at night sitting at the end of their bed. She remembers the chat they had during that TV programme, the laughter and the tears in the ups and downs of family life, the talk she had that summer with her grandad, and the discussions she and her friends had with their youth leader. And suddenly she knows ... deep, deep down in her inmost being ... she has to prove herself to nobody.

In that moment, her hand moves away from the button on her shirt and Alice hears herself say ...

> **No.**

As parents we're playing for that 'No'; but we're also playing for so much more.

As we do the simple things in the everyday ups and downs of family life, we are placing values in our children's hearts. We're equipping them not only to make wise decisions and stay safe, but also to enjoy the wealth of opportunities that the digital age has to offer.

APPENDIX

Further help and support

The following organizations have published helpful advice and guidance on the issues described in this book. Much of this information is for parents, but there are also some helpline contact details for anyone to use. Specific web addresses obviously change from time to time, so you may need to find the article you are looking for by searching from an organization's home page or a general web browser.

❶ Ask About Games
www.askaboutgames.com
Videos and articles on getting the best out of gaming as a family. Advice on how to play games together, as well as which games are suitable for children.

❶ Bullying UK
www.bullying.co.uk
Helpline: 0808 800 2222
Information and advice on bullying specifically, as well as other challenges facing children in the digital world. There is a helpline (free even on mobiles) and live chat.

❶ CEOP (Child Exploitation and Online Protection Centre)
www.ceop.police.uk
Internet safety advice for parents and carers with a 'virtual police station' to report abuse on the Internet. To report concerns that a child is being groomed, or in immediate danger, contact: www.ceop.police.uk/ceop-reporting

❶ Care for the Family
www.careforthefamily.org.uk
A national charity that aims to promote strong family life and help those who face family difficulties. It provides parenting, relationship and bereavement support through events, resources, courses, training and volunteer networks.

ⓘ Childline
www.childline.org.uk
Helpline: 0800 1111
A free twenty-four-hour counselling service for children and young people up to their 19th birthday in the UK, provided by the NSPCC. Childline deals with any issue that causes distress or concern, including online bullying, safety and abuse online.

ⓘ Childnet International
www.childnet.com
Information for children about the latest websites and services they like to use: mobiles, gaming, downloading, social networking and more. A section for parents includes helpful information about what children and young people are doing online, together with useful ways to keep your child safe.

ⓘ Common Sense Media
www.commonsensemedia.org
Information, advice, and innovative tools to help harness the power of media and technology as a positive force in all children's lives.

ⓘ Fight the New Drug
www.fightthenewdrug.org
An excellent, user-friendly website suitable for teenagers and adults. Using videos and interactive articles, FTND explains the damage that pornography does to our brains, our hearts and our society. Backed up by scientific research and powerful testimony, it is a helpful resource for anyone concerned about the issues around pornography.

ⓘ Forcefield
(Download the App)
An app to help parents monitor their children's phone use. Functions include setting a sleep time on your child's device, monitoring the websites they've looked at, and creating settings that block inappropriate content, all of which can be done through the parent's smartphone.

ⓘ Get Safe Online

www.getsafeonline.org

Practical advice on how to protect yourself, your computers and mobile devices, and your business against fraud, identity theft, viruses and other problems encountered online. Includes a specific section on safeguarding children.

ⓘ Headstrong

Beheadstrong.org.uk

An online space for young people looking at how to get the best out of your mind from a Christian faith perspective. Videos, articles and fun stuff covering a broad range of topics linked with mental health and wellbeing.

ⓘ Internet Matters

www.internetmatters.org

Information and advice to help parents keep their children safe online, covering issues such as online bullying, online grooming, inappropriate content, pornography, self-harm.

ⓘ Kidscape

Kidscape.org.uk

Parent advice line: 020 7823 5430

Advice and support for parents, carers and children about bullying that is taking place inside or outside school, or over social platforms and phones.

ⓘ Ollee

https://app.ollee.org.uk/#/

Ollee is a virtual friend created by Parentzone. Children aged 8–11 can interact with him online to help them process their experiences and emotions on a range of subjects including school, family, friends and the Internet. Parents can also use Ollee for advice on the subjects they're concerned their child might be struggling with.

❶ NSPCC

www.nspcc.org.uk
Helpline: 0808 800 5000

A national charity helping children who have been abused to rebuild their lives, protecting those at risk, and finding the best ways of preventing abuse from ever happening. Website includes information and advice about online safety issues.

❶ PAPAYA

www.papayaparents.com

PAPAYA bring groups of parents and children together to make positive, proactive choices regarding smartphone use and social media. They facilitate parents to form groups, as well as running events and visiting schools.

❶ Parent Info

www.parentinfo.org

A broad range of articles advising parents on Internet issues from responsible Instagram use to vlogging. Well-researched, regularly updated and practically helpful, it also includes resources for schools and links to organizations for further help.

❶ Parentzone

www.parentzone.org.uk

General advice on family life with sections on the digital world.

❶ Place2Be

www.place2be.org.uk

A children's mental health charity providing in-school support and expert training to improve the emotional wellbeing of pupils, families, teachers and school staff.

❶ Safer Internet Centre

www.saferinternet.org.uk

Advice and support on online safety issues, including an anonymous hotline to report and remove child sexual abuse imagery and videos wherever they are found in the world. There is also a helpline for professionals working with children and young people with online safety issues.

ⓘ Taming Gaming

www.patreon.com/taminggaming

Andy Robertson produces weekly video-newsletters to help parents actively guide their children's gaming and screen time. 'Taming Gaming' the book is also available (unbound.com/books/taming-gaming/).

ⓘ The Naked Truth Project

www.thenakedtruthproject.com

Practical support, resources and workshops to tackle the damaging impact of pornography, including an online guide for parents. *www.ntruth.education*

Information on Naked Truth's school lessons and parental workshops. (A good resource to pass on to teachers.)

ⓘ Thinkuknow

www.thinkuknow.co.uk

A range of helpful information for children, young people, parents, carers and professionals, including games and advice for specific age groups.

ⓘ Vodafone Digital Parenting

www.vodafone.com/content/digital-parenting.html

Advice, support, and practical 'how to' guides for keeping your children safe online.

ⓘ Young Minds

www.youngminds.org.uk
Helpline for parents: 0808 802 5544
Helpline for parents: 0800 802 5544
YoungMinds Crisis Messenger: Text YM 85258

Free, 24/7 help and support for children, parents and professionals concerning mental health issues.

❶ Youthscape
www.youthscape.co.uk
Youthscape exists to give young people the best social, emotional and spiritual landscape on which to build their lives and achieve their potential. The website includes resources, research, advice and details of their programmes.

Specific Information

❶ Checking your child's web history
https://famiguard.imyfone.com/track/browser-history-tracker/

❶ Family Internet agreements
www.childnet.com/blog/family-agreement
www.wisekids.org.uk/wisekidsacceptableuse.pdf

❶ Parental controls and filters
www.Internetmatters.org/parental-controls/interactive-guide
www.childnet.com/parents-and-carers/hot-topics/parental-controls

❶ Video games ratings: age and content
www.pegi.info

❶ Removing abusive posts
www.thinkuknow.co.uk/14_plus/help/Contact-social-sites
www.bullying.co.uk/cyberbullying/what-to-do-if-you-re-beingbullied-on-a-social-network

❶ Guides to children's apps, games and sites
www.commonsensemedia.org
www.net-aware.org.uk
Talking to children about online safety, privacy sexting, porn and grooming.

❶ NSPCC – Keeping Children Safe section
https://www.nspcc.org.uk/keeping-children-safe/online-safety/